LET NOT MAN PUT
Asunder

S LYNN G

XULON PRESS

Xulon Press
2301 Lucien Way #415
Maitland, FL 32751
407.339.4217
www.xulonpress.com

© 2018 by S Lynn G

All rights reserved solely by the author. The author guarantees all contents are original and do not infringe upon the legal rights of any other person or work. No part of this book may be reproduced in any form without the permission of the author. The views expressed in this book are not necessarily those of the publisher.

Unless otherwise indicated, Scripture quotations taken from the King James Version (KJV) – *public domain*.

Printed in the United States of America.

ISBN-13: 978-1-54565-096-7

Table of Contents

Preface v
Dedication. vii

1. Humpty Dumpty. 1
2. Sat on a Wall 12
3. Had a Great Fall 20
4. All the Kings Horses and All the Kings Men 48
5. Couldn't Put Humpty Together Again... 48
6. But God Can 58
7. A Checklist for Marriage. 78

The Plan of Salvation 89

Preface

I have listened to many ladies describe the end results of their divorce. I certainly understand and can easily sympathize with them because I too have struggled through a divorce and an annulment.

All of the information contained in this book is based on my personal experiences, and as you read, I pray you will keep an open heart. This is not a magical or cure-all book, but hopefully it will lead you to a greater understanding of how God's Word can guide you through the challenging maze of married life.

Divorce is both devastating and destructive. The Bible says in *Jeremiah 17:9, "The heart is deceitful above all things, and desperately wicked: who can know it?"* The answer to that question is found in *Jeremiah 17:10a, "I the LORD search the heart...."* So like it or not, the fact is, God knows our hearts, thoughts, and motives.

God established the institution of marriage in the Garden of Eden and did not intend for marriage to end in divorce. When a man and a woman declare their vows of marriage, God is involved; therefore, one of Satan's primary objectives is to destroy a marriage that might bring glory to God.

Married couples will not always agree on everything. Without a doubt, the annoying idiosyncrasies they both possess will find a way to press on that last frayed nerve at times, so be aware that pride or the desire to be the one in control is the first step to destroying your marriage. *"Can two walk together, except they be agreed?" (Amos 3:3).* The Bible says, *"... if a house be divided against itself, that house cannot stand" (Mark 3:25).*

So what should you do if your marriage is falling apart? Who can you turn to for advice without fear of chastisement or blame? What should you do if you or your children are being abused mentally, physically, or sexually by your spouse or live-in partner? Ask yourself, would God want me to stay in that type of relationship?

Although you will not find within the pages of this book all of the answers for the circumstances you are facing nor the answers to specific questions you have. However, you will find Scriptural solutions and principles learned from years of experience and you will find out what the Bible says about salvation.

The word *saved* means a person who has accepted Jesus Christ as personal Savior; that person is a <u>born again</u> Christian, a child of God, *saved* by grace and on his or her way to Heaven. Hallelujah!

The word *unsaved* means that a person's natural born sin nature has separated him or her from God. Jesus said in **John 3:3,** *"...Verily, verily, I say unto thee, Except a man be born again, he cannot see the kingdom of God."* So...if you have not accepted Jesus Christ as Savior, you will not see the kingdom of God but are on the way to Hell. Yikes!

By the way... it is that same natural born sin nature that is the biggest threat to marriage. However, because Jesus paid our sin debt in full on the Cross, He alone can be our Savior. His Word also tells us how to get us through the rough areas in our marriage.

The resurrection from the tomb declares that Jesus is God and that He has THE POWER that you will need again and again when dealing with problems in your marriage. A Christ-centered marriage is vitally important.

Dedication

To my husband, who was willing to allow me to include his involvement in this devastating chapter of our lives.

To my entire family for allowing me to put in print my personal shame that has ultimately affected their lives in many ways.

To my friends, who were willing to take time to listen and offer their endless encouragement.

To my fabulous friend Rena Fish, for providing her expertise and endurance while demonstrating the patience of Job as she edited not only this book, but three others for me. I am very grateful for my Pastor Mark Chappell, and friends, Ethelyn Martin, Mindy Holeman, Pastor Pack, and my youngest sister Kathy Embry for their valuable input as well.

It was only by God's grace that I was able to complete this book because I was willing to quit so many times.

I thank God for all of you and am very blessed by your friendship and love.

Chapter 1

Humpty Dumpty...

Humpty Dumpty sat on a wall,

Humpty Dumpty had a great fall.

All the king's horses and all the king's men,

Couldn't put Humpty together again.

My family moved across the street from my future husband (Humpty) the summer of 1961, just before I (Dumpty) turned twelve. Humpty's sister and I became instant best friends and finished grade school together in the same class; we were inseparable for those two remaining years of grade school. I remember that I was not attracted to Humpty when I first met him (or any other boy for that matter). I still thought boys were creepy. I remember that I had, at my mother's insistence, recently and very reluctantly given up playing with dolls around that time, so the thought of dating or marriage was the farthest thing from my mind.

The summer before I started high school in 1963, my parents were out for the evening. So when a friend of mine stopped by, two of my sisters and I stepped out into the front yard to visit with her. We were having a great time when my friend pulled some cigarettes out of her pocket and asked if we wanted one as she passed the pack around. We all accepted, and we all lit up. Not one of us gave a thought as to who might be watching. After all, it was dark outside, and the adults were gone, so what was the harm…right?

I found out the next day that the neighbors were watching our every move and listening to our conversation. The next morning two of those neighbor ladies promptly told my mother what we had been up to in her absence, and I can still recall that dreaded and well-known "Wait till your father gets home" statement, which revealed what was in store for my sisters and me. My sisters each got their punishment, and then I received a severe beating because it was my friend and I should have known better.

My parents both smoked. In fact, as children we were sent to the store to buy them their cigarettes. I guess this is where that old adage "Do as I say, not as I do" comes into play. (Wow! What example are you setting for your children?) Obviously, my life at home was not all it should have been.

As I left grade school and entered into high school, my attention became divided between my best friend and her brother Humpty. High school was a new world to me: meeting so many new people, changing rooms for each class, having to run across campus, carrying all those heavy books. As freshmen, Humpty's sister and I found it impossible to make it to our lockers, located in a remote corner of the eastern wing of the campus, to drop off our books and still make it to class on time. So when Humpty, a senior, offered to let his sister and me use his more conveniently located locker in between classes, we gladly took him up on his offer.

I had no idea that using that locker would eventually lead to Humpty's carrying my books and walking me to my classes every day. And get a load of this...before I knew it, we were having lunch together. Even though our lunch usually consisted of Twinkies, Lays Potato Chips, and a Coca-Cola, we didn't care. It was enough for us because we were spending time together. Before that year was out, Humpty invited his sister and me to ride to school with him instead of walking. What a treat! As summer approached, that half-mile walk to school was very hot, and of course winter could be very cold, but rainy days were the worst. So of course we said yes to that offer too. What a guy! He was so nice—and he had a great sense of humor.

Near the end of my freshman year, Humpty came up with the idea of ditching school and going to the lake. It was a hot day, school was so boring, and a day at the lake sounded like so much fun. Humpty, his sister, and their next-door neighbor were going, and they wanted me to go too. But...I remembered that beating I had gotten for smoking the summer before. So I said, "No, I am not going." But...the more they talked about going, the more enticed I was. Besides, who was going to know? I would be home before my parents got home from work, so I gave in and went to the lake.

When I got home, I started in with my chores, thinking about all the fun we had enjoyed at the lake until three of our fun-loving foursome told me the school had called their parents and ratted us out. Boy was I in luck! We didn't have a phone, and if we would have had one, no one was at home to answer that call. So I was still in the clear! That is, until our neighbor (the same neighbor who informed my mom about the smoking incident) summoned me to come talk to her. She asked me if I had ditched school with the others. I admitted that I had.

The word *yikes* didn't cover what was going through my mind when she said I should tell my parents when they got home about my ditching school that day. She said it would be better coming from me than coming from the school. So once again I had made a choice to be disobedient that would bring consequences. I knew better than to ditch school, but I had let others influence me. ***Galatians 6:7, "Be not deceived; God is not mocked: for whatsoever a man soweth, that shall he also reap."***

I had just a few minutes to get my thoughts together before my mom pulled into the driveway. I figured if I told my mom without my dad around, she might have mercy on me, and dad would never have to know. But she was still yelling at me when he walked in the door. Then she said, "Now you can tell your dad what you just told me!" I told on myself and received the beating of a lifetime. Recovery took three days, and on top of that, I wasn't allowed to ride or walk to school with the other three of our foursome for the rest of that school year. The other three were only yelled at and couldn't associate with each other for a few weeks.

In the summer of 1964, our fun foursome spent some time together, but after finding new interests and different friends, we pretty much drifted apart, with the exception of Humpty and me. Having permission from my parents, I went to the lake with Humpty, his sister, and their older, married brothers and their families. However, most of the summer, I was either babysitting, or my sisters and I were confined to the house.

That same summer our family moved just before school started. Instead of living across the street from Humpty, my back yard butted up to a field that butted up to Humpty's back yard. My family's move still had me in a house that was on the way to school, so it didn't interfere with my walking or riding to school with Humpty.

My sophomore year of high school consisted of so many changes. Humpty had a few morning classes to make up in order to get his diploma, so once again he allowed his sister and me to share his conveniently located locker. Just like the year before, he carried my books and walked me to my classes for the first half of the school year.

Then...the morning of April 1, 1965, when I should have been at school, I was standing in my living room breaking the news to my mother that I was pregnant. She was broken hearted, and this time she did have compassion on me, telling me not come home for a few days so my father would have time to adjust to the news that his fifteen-year-old daughter was going to have a baby.

There were no wedding plans, beautiful white dress, or guests galore. Back then a *shotgun wedding* was the term used to describe the brief ceremony—only my mother, Humpty's father, and the both of us standing before a judge. I can tell you there was nothing beautiful or romantic attached to that situation.

Our honeymoon was spent in the bedroom belonging to the children of my new brother and sister-in-law. The only income we had was the paper route my eighteen-year-old husband had, and the only thing I can say about the car we owned was that it still ran. The future looked pretty grim, but we had each other, and nothing else mattered (or so we thought).

When my father finally got over the fact that I had disappointed him and that he was going to be a grandfather, he calmed down and got my husband a job at the cattle feed lot where he worked. We then were able to rent a little travel trailer. Things were looking up for us, and we still had each other.

When I got married, I thought my husband and I would raise our children, enjoy our grandchildren, and grow old together; I expected our marriage vows to be the lifetime commitment that God intended them to be. However, like Humpty Dumpty, I had a great fall. My marriage was blindsided by an attack from Satan. My hopes and dreams were certainly shattered: every part of my life was definitely broken into a million pieces, never to be put back together again. Just so you know, neither my husband nor I knew the Lord and Savior personally when we got married. Nope. We were nothing but lost sinners on our way to an eternal Hell.

God established the institution of marriage in the Garden of Eden, just after Adam named all of the animals, the fowl of the air, and every beast of the field; *"... **but for Adam there was not found an help meet for him. And the LORD God caused*** *a deep sleep to fall upon Adam, and he slept: and he took one of his ribs, and closed up the flesh instead thereof; And the rib, which the LORD God had taken from man, made he a woman, and brought her unto the man. And Adam said, This is now bone of my bones, and flesh of my flesh: she shall be called Woman, because she was taken out of Man. Therefore shall a man leave his father and his mother, and shall cleave unto his wife: and they shall be one flesh. And they were both naked, the man and his wife, and were not ashamed" (Genesis 2:20-25).*

When a born again Christian declares his/her wedding vows, God is involved in that marriage. But... that is not so in the marriage of the unsaved, meaning those who have not accepted Christ as Savior. God will not force His way into the marriage of a man and a woman who have not accepted His Son as Savior. God will wait until they have accepted Christ through salvation to become involved in their marriage, and God has no intention that any marriage end in divorce. *"Wherefore they are no more twain, but one flesh. What therefore God hath joined together, let not man put asunder" (Matthew 19:6).*

Because our thoughts are not God's thoughts, we have a tendency to ignore God and His plan for marriage. **Psalms 10:4** says, *"The wicked, through the pride of his countenance, will not seek after God: God is not in all his thoughts."* We fail to recognize that God knows our heart better than we do. The Bible says, *"The heart is deceitful above all things, and desperately wicked: who can know it? I the LORD search the heart..." (Jeremiah 17:9* and **10a**).

The society we live in is so different from God's plan. It's all turned around. There are few morals, and like animals, men and women are only concerned with satisfying themselves. In direct opposition to the philosophy of this world, God has always intended for both the man and the woman to be pure when they enter into marriage. *Hebrews 13:4, "Marriage is honourable in all, and the bed undefiled: but whoremongers and adulterers God will judge."*

Lust is a false substitute for love. Lust is satisfying one's own selfish desires and is totally void of respect and definitely without security or future. It is impossible to have a loving relationship in a marriage without trust and honesty, which produce security, reliance, and hope for the future. Because of our sinful nature, our heart can easily confuse us and lead us astray. Therefore, we are instructed to ***"Trust in the LORD with all thine heart; and lean not unto thine own understanding" (Proverbs 3:5).***

Were your wedding vows the more traditional ones similar to this, "I...promise you...to have and to hold from this day forward, for better or for worse, for richer, for poorer, in sickness and in health, to love, honor, and to cherish, until death do us part"? Or did you and your spouse write your own vows? If so, did those vows sound anything like this: "My lust for you is burning out of control, and when that flame goes out, so will I"? Doesn't that sound ridiculous? Yet that is exactly the thinking that some people bring into the marriage. They will promise to be faithful forever while thinking, *If this doesn't work out, I can get a divorce.* ***"Then when lust hath conceived, it bringeth forth sin: and sin, when it is finished, bringeth forth death" (James 1:15).*** The word *death* does not have to mean the death of a person. One of the synonyms to *death* is *end*, and according to the Encarta Dictionary, *end* means "downfall, ruin, and collapse." So "...sin, when it is finished, bringeth forth death" very well could mean the collapse, downfall, ruin, or end of your marriage.

In all honesty, you aren't assuming that by repeating your marriage vows happiness will automatically follow you the rest of your life with little or no effort on your part, are you? I did. What about the words *for worse ... for poorer ... in sickness?* None of those words spell blissful happiness. Did you really mean "until death do us part" or just until the flame goes out? As a newlywed, in spite of youth and lack of finances, I was convinced that nothing could extinguish the flame of our love. I just knew we would be the exception to the rule.

All sin is against God. The Bible clearly states in *Exodus 20:14, "Thou shalt not commit adultery."* However, adultery is usually not a single step. There is a natural progression of sin that starts as a thought and leads a person down the pathway of more sin. We cannot excuse the "small" sins, such as those little white lies, being sneaky or deceptive in not telling your spouse about a text you received, stealing time away from your family, or discussing the faults of your spouse behind his or her back to make yourself look better—just to name a few. *Mark 7:21* says, *"For from within, out of the heart of men, proceed evil thoughts, adulteries, fornications, murders."*

As time goes on...and the wedding vows are forgotten... and when married life isn't meeting your expectations...let's stop right there for a moment. The word *forgotten* is the first thing to consider. It is when you forget the promise you made to your spouse that the real trouble begins. That's when you are no longer honest, no longer dependable, and no longer trustworthy. You are still responsible for your own actions even when your spouse fails you.

There is a rather unique conversation that takes place between Jesus and the Pharisees in *Mark 10:2-9: "The Pharisees came to him [Jesus], and asked him, Is it lawful for a man to put away his wife? tempting him [Jesus]. And he [Jesus] answered and said unto them [the Pharisees], What did Moses command you? And they [the Pharisees] said, Moses suffered to write a bill of divorcement, and to put her away. And Jesus answered and said unto them, For the hardness of your heart he wrote you this precept. But from the beginning of the creation God made them male and female. For this cause shall a man leave his father and mother, and cleave to his wife; And they twain shall be one flesh: so then they are no more twain, but one flesh. What therefore God hath joined together, let not man put asunder."*

Although divorce was not God's original intent, the Bible does not use the word *hate* in reference to divorce. However, the word *hate* is used in regards to "putting away." *Malachi*

2:15* and *16* says, *"...Therefore take heed to your spirit, and let none deal treacherously against the wife of his youth. For the LORD, the God of Israel, saith that he hateth putting away: for one covereth violence with his garment, saith the LORD of hosts: therefore take heed to your spirit, that ye deal not treacherously." Divorce doesn't happen overnight; the process of "putting away" includes unkindness, laziness, lying, deceitfulness, and unfaithfulness. And I believe it all starts with selfishness. God hates the treachery that leads to divorce. ***Proverbs 4:23* says, *"Keep thy heart with all diligence; for out of it are the issues of life."***

The Encarta Dictionary states the definition of *divorce* as, "to end a marriage to somebody by an official decision in a court of law." Well, YIKES! That sounds so matter of fact, cold, and unfeeling, like somehow the lives of the people involved will not be affected or changed in any devastating way at all. The definition should include the suffering, heartache, sorrow, fear, anger, and depression that will inevitably flare up at the most inopportune times. The definition of *divorce* is way too simple. Divorce changes lives forever, very much like Humpty Dumpty who couldn't be put back together again.

- **Questions to think about:**

1. What is your marriage based on? Love or lust? List your thoughts.

   _____
   _____
   _____
   _____
   _____
   _____

2. If you are not married, are you really ready to make a serious commitment to a marriage, or are you just looking for a way out of your current situation? If you are already married, are you taking your marriage commitment seriously, or are you just looking for a way out of your current situation?

   _____
   _____
   _____
   _____
   _____
   _____

3. Have you prayed and asked God for His guidance? Take time right now to write down the specific areas in which you need His guidance. Spend time in prayer concerning these areas.

   _____
   _____
   _____
   _____
   _____
   _____

- **Verses to memorize:**

  1. *Proverbs 3:5-7, "Trust in the LORD with all thine heart; and lean not unto thine own understanding. In all thy ways acknowledge him, and he shall direct thy paths. Be not wise in thine own eyes: fear the LORD, and depart from evil."*

  2. *Mark 10:9, "What therefore God hath joined together, let not man put asunder."*

- **Passages to read:**

  Ephesians 5
  Genesis 1 and 2

Chapter 2

Sat on a Wall ...

Satan wants nothing more than he wants to discredit God's Word, and he has many different and subtle approaches to accomplish his goal. One of Satan's primary objectives is to destroy any marriage that might bring glory to God. That is why we are to *"Be sober, be vigilant; because your adversary the devil, as a roaring lion, walketh about, seeking whom he may devour" (1 Peter 5:8).*

The word sober means "to be clear-minded and serious," and vigilant means "to be paying attention and cautious." The warning in 1 Peter 5:8 is given so that you will know for certain that Satan is trying not only to destroy your marriage but also to devour you and your entire family. Is your guard up? Are you clear-minded and paying attention to what is going on in your home and with your family? Or are you allowing Satan to desensitize your household one inconspicuous compromise at a time through the variety of media available today, which promote all types of promiscuity?

Most of the television programs and much of the content that is available on the internet can only be described as appalling. The vast majority of the programs on television are wicked and disgraceful. Do you really want your children watching them? The internet is worse because immoral content, including pornography, can be viewed privately by those of all ages. Children in grade school can take x-rated selfies on their cell phones, pass them around to their friends, and post them on the internet to be viewed by strangers, not giving any thought to the fact that those images can never be erased. It is not uncommon to hear of a marriage ending in divorce because of a lustful romance that started in an internet chatroom or by means of a dating app. ...

Television programs depict situations that excuse infidelity, fornication, outrageous anger flair-ups, and murder. For instance, when you turn on your favorite television program—spouse sitting beside you and children at your feet, eyes glued to the television, living in the moment of somebody's made-up life—that is when the seeds of compromise are planted. We have allowed our eyes and ears to put thoughts in our minds, and sooner or later those thoughts will be put into actions.

To help you understand what is really happening, consider the following: the next time you are watching a program that includes a sexual encounter, if it does not make you feel the least bit uncomfortable, know that you have already been desensitized. Try not to be offended as I ask you a few questions. How would you feel if you invited some friends over for dinner, and after dinner when everyone was relaxing in the living room, all of a sudden your friends started making out, then began taking their clothes off with the intention of having sex right there in front of you? Would you allow that to happen? I would be horrified if you even considered allowing such a thing. So what is the difference between watching strangers have sex on television and watching your friends have sex in person? Both would be taking place in your living room.

The next question is, would you invite your children into your bedroom to watch you have sex? No, of course you wouldn't! Then why would it be acceptable for them to watch a sexual act on television? Such programs are the introduction to pornography, which only leads to disaster later in life. Watching provocative sexual images peaks a curiosity in the minds of young children and sets them on a path to investigation of and engaging in sex at a very early age, which often leads to teen pregnancy. It is even more mind-boggling to think what might be spinning around in the mind of your spouse while watching such programs. Is this really what you want for your children, your spouse, or yourself?

Most of the music that is going out over the airwaves is so vulgar and loud that it removes all purity and wholesomeness, yet we allow our children to listen to it. Surely an innocent baby would find it most difficult to sleep under such conditions. Apartment dwellers can find the sanctity of their home invaded by the over powering, pulsating beat that vibrates the walls and rattles the dishes.

Music is everywhere: shopping malls, grocery stores, elevators, doctor's offices, even in our homes and cars. The truth is, most of the so-called music of today isn't even music. It is someone else's anger and frustration being voiced with vulgar sexual references, the worst profanity ever, and blatant promotion of drug use. Because music is directly connected to our emotions, we need to be careful of the music we choose to listen to.

Music was created by God to bring glory to Himself. Lucifer, aka Satan, sang in Heaven's choir before he got the bright idea that he could be like the Most High God. Because of Lucifer's pride, he was kicked right out of Heaven. Satan is the Prince of the Power of the Air, and he wants to rob God of the glory our Creator deserves. Satan uses his deceitful ways to manipulate us into thinking that we too can be like God through our pride, doing whatever we want to do—but the Bible says differently. ***Ephesians 6:12, "For we wrestle not against flesh and blood, but against principalities, against powers, against the rulers of the darkness of this world, against spiritual wickedness in high places."*** Ungodly music plants wrong thoughts and desires in the minds of the listeners. Remember, every seed planted in our mind will eventually produce an action.

Music should be a beautiful blend of melody, harmony, and rhythm that is pleasing to the ear. An overpowering beat negatively affects our heartbeat and can eventually damage our hearing. Lucifer's music sends wrong messages. Eventually the listener will believe that drugs, alcohol, and illicit sex are acceptable. What we see and hear repeatedly soon become normal to us and to our children. When we allow ungodly influences to come into our homes, we have given our approval without saying one single word. *"For we cannot but speak the things which we have seen and heard." (Acts 4:20).* Satan will use whatever approach he can to destroy families and marriages. The Bible says in *Proverbs 4:23, "Keep thy heart with all diligence; for out of it are the issues of life."*

I know music had an influence on my marriage. My husband and I listened to country and western music; we even went dancing with our friends to the popular honky-tonks. Of course, that meant drinking alcohol and dancing with each other's spouses. I have no idea if you are familiar with that type of music, but I can tell you that the words to most of those songs are whining and complaining about a wrecked marriage and wanting a lost spouse back. Of the friends we went dancing with, every single one of us had a marriage that ended in divorce. Two of the couple's divorces were brought on by a husband who had an affair with his best friend's wife.

Satan is aggressively using the internet to destroy marriages and minds. He is not age- discriminatory. The only protection for our families and our marriages is for us to pay close attention to the things of God rather than allowing Satan to influence our way of thinking. Men, women, and children are spending hours on the internet watching pornography. Pornography will jeopardize not only your marriage but the future marriages of your children. *Ezekiel 12:2, "Son of man, thou dwellest in the midst of a rebellious house, which have eyes to see, and see not; they have ears to hear, and hear not: for they are a rebellious house."* The things we choose to see and hear should bring glory to God. *Joshua 24:15, "And if it seem evil unto you to serve the LORD, choose you this day whom ye will serve...but as for me and my house, we will serve the LORD."*

Another method Satan uses to target marriage is to confuse the roles that God established in the Garden. Remember that in Genesis 2:20, God used one of Adam's ribs to create Eve so she could be a helper to Adam. I have heard it said from the pulpit that God used a rib bone instead of a foot bone so Eve could walk as a companion by Adam's side and not as a slave under his foot. Of course, the Bible does not state this specifically, but it makes sense and could certainly be used as a reminder that we are to treat our spouses with respect. *Ephesians 4:32, "And be ye kind one to another, tenderhearted, forgiving one another, even as God for Christ's sake hath forgiven you."*

When a husband and wife do not respect each other, all respect leaves the entire household. Keep in mind that as parents, we are teaching our children every minute of every day. So...what are we teaching our children? Often certain types of sin are prevalent in a family history, and these can be passed down from one generation to another. Such family sins need to be identified as destructive and should not be considered the norm. Are there generational sins in your family that need to be recognized? Will you be the one to break the hold of these sins on your family, or will you allow them to be passed on?

When a woman usurps her husband's authority, she is in disobedience toward God. This is not to say that her husband cannot give her charge over certain areas that may lighten his load; however, for her to take charge on her own because he is lazy or selfish will cause contention and resentment. Role reversal is a destroyer to any marriage. When a man is too lazy or selfish to fulfill his responsibilities, the wife will feel the need to step in and take over the leadership of the family to the detriment of their household.

When a man chooses to abandon his leadership, he not only disrupts the natural roles of the marriage, but he also sets himself up for future potential catastrophe. Both financial ramifications and other effects on the family dynamic can be disastrous.

Sat on a Wall ...

- **Questions to think about:**

1. List the names of the people who are affected by the music, television and internet exposure you allow in your home. Be sure to list extended family members, friends, co-workers and others you have influence over.

_____
_____
_____
_____
_____
_____
_____

2. Are you thinking clearly and seriously paying attention to what is going on in your home and with your family? Make a check list of things that need to be changed based on God's Word.

_____
_____
_____
_____
_____
_____
_____
_____

3. Remember that those in your home are watching, listening, and participating in the same things you are. How are you influencing them? Make a list of the things that you think are influencing them in a good way and those things that may be influencing them in a wrong way.

_____
_____
_____
_____
_____
_____

4. Wife, have you taken over the leadership of your family? If yes, be honest and list the reasons why. Then ask God to show you through His Word your proper position in your marriage.

_____
_____
_____
_____
_____
_____
_____

- **Verses to memorize:**

    1. *Ephesians 5:22-26, "Wives, submit yourselves unto your own husbands, as unto the Lord. For the husband is the head of the wife, even as Christ is the head of the church: and he is the saviour of the body. Therefore as the church is subject unto Christ, so let the wives be to their own husbands in everything. Husbands, love your wives, even as Christ also loved the church, and gave himself for it. That he might sanctify and cleanse it with the washing of the water by the word."*

    2. *1 Peter 5:8, "Be sober, be vigilant; because your adversary the devil, as a roaring lion, walketh about, seeking whom he may devour."*

    3. *Acts 4:20, "For we cannot but speak the things which we have seen and heard."*

- **Passages to read:**

    Ephesians 5

Chapter 3

Had a Great Fall …

After my husband and I had been married only five years, he didn't want to be married anymore. Long before my husband informed me of his decision, we had entered into the battleground of disagreements. One particular time as my husband was backing out of our gravel driveway, rocks and dirt flying everywhere, I was thinking, *That does it!* While he was still backing up, I grabbed a handful of gravel and threw it at the car in total frustration. As big of a hurry as he had seemed to be in, who knew he would stop the car just as the gravel arrived. The windshield looked as though it had been fired upon by a machine gun. This fight and many others escalated out of control, the result of actions and reactions brought on by accusations and suspicions, taking all the respect out of the relationship to the point of loathing even the sight of one another. How could we have changed so quickly from the point of thinking that our love was all that mattered?

In spite of the turmoil in my life, I wanted nothing to do with the religious crowd. In my mind, I saw born again Christians as hypocrites, and in my prideful thinking I said, "Thanks, but no thanks" to all of them. I can honestly tell you that I was not seeking God when He found me in a heap of soggy tissues and still sobbing quietly under my broken, and very hardened heart. However, I would later learn that the born again Christians had the very hope I needed.

This may be hard to believe, but the sin of pride is the beginning of the end of all types of relationships, including marriage. Now if you don't think so, God's Word tells us that, *"Pride goeth before destruction, and an haughty spirit before a fall" (Proverbs 16:18).* Notice the Encarta Dictionary definition of *pride*: "self-importance, arrogance, smugness." The definition of *self-importance* is "superiority, haughtiness, conceit." The definition of *smugness* is "self-righteousness." If we are honest with ourselves, we must admit that we all struggle with the sin of pride. And if you don't think so, consider **Proverbs 13:10a, *"Only by pride cometh contention."*** The word *contention* includes arguments, disagreements, conflicts, bickering, and disputes.

Interestingly enough, *humility* is the antonym to all those words I looked up. *Humility* is meekness and modesty all rolled into one. Those characteristics are very important to have in all relationships, especially your marriage, because they allow you to work every situation out in a quiet and civil manner without tempers flaring out of control.

The *Webster's Elementary Dictionary for Boys and Girls* defines *pride* as "proud or haughty behavior; disdain." I looked up *disdain* in the same dictionary, and I think everyone will understand this definition best: "contempt, derision, and disregard." When used as a verb, *disdain* means "to scorn, hold in contempt, look down on." Last but not least, "to disparage." The definition of *disparage* gives a vivid picture we all need to take a closer look at. It means "to belittle, ridicule, criticize, run down, sneer at, and vilify."

Criticism is a great way to ruin your marriage and surely comes from a prideful attitude; however, you may want to memorize ***James 4:6*** as a helpful reminder of the importance of humility, ***"God resisteth the proud, but giveth grace unto*** *the humble."* Respect and praise will allow you to get through the difficult times much faster and will be less stressful on your entire family.

As dangerous as a communicable disease, divorce can spread like wildfire, infecting the minds of those who are already in an unstable marriage. Just the word *divorce* plants the seed of an unrealistic, effortless escape from the unresolved day-to-day conflicts that have gotten out of control through pride, stubbornness, and obvious immaturity.

Married couples will not always agree on everything. Without a doubt, the annoying idiosyncrasies they both possess will find a way to press on that last frayed nerve at times, but they cannot let pride or the desire to be the one in control get in the way of coming to an agreement that suits them both. Having the power to control your spouse is not love. The fact is, it is just the opposite. True love is expressed through respect, courtesy, honesty, and commitment.

When the Lord God formed Adam out of the dust of the earth and He breathed the breath of life into his nostrils, Adam became a living soul. ***"And the LORD God said, "It is not good that the man should be alone; I will make him an help meet for him" (Genesis 2:18).*** That help meet's name was Eve. I wonder if God sat them down and said, "Now, Adam, I am putting you in charge of everything; you are to be the leader of your home." Oh, I really wish I could have been there because I have a feeling that Adam might have jumped up and said, "Hey! Wait just a minute here. I have to be in charge of everything? What about Eve? Doesn't she have to do anything?"—only to have God reply, "Yes, Adam, Eve's job is to help you."

God told Adam in **Genesis 2:17** that he could eat freely from every tree in the garden with one exception: ***"But of the tree of the knowledge of good and evil, thou shalt not eat of it: for in the day that thou eatest thereof thou shalt surely die."*** Because Adam was put in charge, part of his responsibility was protecting his wife. Although Adam did tell Eve about God's command, the Bible does not indicate that Adam said anything to discourage Eve from eating the fruit when the serpent tempted her. And not only that, Adam relinquished his leadership role by willingly following his wife into sin by eating the fruit that she offered to him. *1 Timothy 2:14* says, *"Adam was not deceived, but the woman being deceived was in the transgression."*

God's plan was for Adam and Eve to be the perfect team. Adam was to be the leader, and Eve was to be his helper. The key to having a successful marriage is following God's pattern as expressed in 1 Peter chapter 3.

- *1 Peter 3:1, "Likewise, ye wives, be in subjection to your own husbands; that, if any obey not the word, they also may without the word be won by the conversation of the wives."*

- *1 Peter 3:7, "Likewise, ye husbands, dwell with them according to knowledge, giving honour unto the wife, as unto the weaker vessel, and as being heirs together of the grace of life; that your prayers be not hindered."*

When Adam and Eve sinned and stopped following God's pattern for their marriage, selfishness and conflict entered into their relationship.

Divorce is the ultimate act of selfishness. Walking away from the person we have promised to spend the rest of our life with is a despicable, callous, and costly decision. Are we willing to lose everything and everyone we claim to love? What are we teaching our children through our prideful selfishness and lack of consideration? Certainly not integrity. Our children learn by seeing, hearing, and following the examples we set before them.

I know a lady who used the word *divorce* in front of her husband and children on a regular basis. When her personal income surpassed that of her husband's, she selfishly filed for divorce after 20 years of marriage. She had no problem ripping her family apart because the grass looked greener on the other side of the fence. But little did she realize the commitment that is involved in getting that greener grass to grow. Green grass always involves hard work. Sometimes it involves fertilizer—which usually stinks. Lawn care is time-consuming and expensive, not to mention the back-breaking work of pulling weeds or the dangers of using poison for the stubborn ones. Water is absolutely essential to having that lush green grass your heart desires. Let's not forget about the need for aerating or sometimes calling in a professional. Unfortunately, this lady carried her selfishness with her across the fence.

Keeping a marriage together requires continuous work. Running away from a failing one is not the answer because you take yourself with you everywhere you go. Your unscrupulous spouse is not the only problem in your marriage; even if your spouse "starts it," you have a responsibility for how you respond, relate, or retaliate.

What should you do if you are an abused spouse or if your children are being abused mentally, physically, or sexually? Ask yourself, would God want me to stay in that type of relationship? Sometimes a wise and proper response may be to seek a place of safety for you and your children.

Without question, we have all sinned, and I for one was surprised to learn that when we sin, it is always against God. When King David committed adultery with Bathsheba, he admitted to God, *"Against thee, thee only, have I sinned, and done this evil in thy sight..." (Psalm 51:4).* So many times we forget, if we were even aware of this knowledge, that *"... we wrestle not against flesh and blood, but against principalities, against powers, against the rulers of the darkness of this world, against spiritual wickedness in high places" (Ephesians 6:12).*

Lucifer, through his pride and arrogance, thought he would place himself above Almighty God. Yikes! Can you imagine even thinking such a thought? To be quite honest, we do think those thoughts. The seven deadly sins are found in Proverbs

6:16-19, and the first one listed is a proud look. Anytime a person is trying to elevate himself into a position of control, he thinks he knows more than God. However, God sees all, hears all, knows all, and is in control of all. ***Proverbs 16:5*** says, ***"Every one that is proud in heart is an abomination to the LORD: though hand join in hand, he shall not be unpunished."*** Allowing pride, instead of God, to control our thoughts and choices guarantees a fall worse than that of Humpty Dumpty's.

Because God designed marriage, there is no room for selfishness, dishonesty, or deception in a marriage relationship. Marriage should never be entered into with the thought of divorce as a solution to problems; there is no quick fix. I have suffered the loss of many things in my life, as most people have, but the broken heart of divorce has been the hardest for me to endure. The pain started everywhere all at once and filled my heart full of agony and fear.

I am overwhelmed with grief, heartache, and sorrow when I think about how easy it is for someone to make the careless decision of divorce that will affect the future of countless people, especially the children. Don't fool yourself; divorce is never ending. The long-lasting consequences can be exhausting not only because you will have to contend with the repercussions, but also because many times counselors, therapists, preachers, and other family members are called in to help those that are deeply involved and affected by your divorce, even long after you have moved on....

I personally do not believe that divorce is the answer to any marital problem a couple may be facing right now or in the future. However, I do believe that unresolved, pre-existing situations brought into a marriage either by the husband, wife, or both can end in divorce as a result of pride and stubbornness as those pre-existing situations are exposed over a period of time.

Without being rude or sounding snooty, may I remind you once again that pride is the root cause of divorce. Think about the word root for a moment. One of the many meanings of *root* is "the fundamental cause, basis, or essence of something or the source from which something derives." The Bible says in ***Proverbs 13:10a, "Only by pride cometh contention."*** I don't know of any divorce that did not begin with arguing, disagreeing, and quarrelling. Contention then leads to discontentment.

Discontentment means that a person is not happy with the way things are going, opening the door for pride to accelerate the contention. Does this sound familiar? "I am tired of it all; I am not going to put up with this nonsense anymore." Pride causes the tug of war to intensify the conflict, and pride can nourish the idea of divorce.

Once married, the two partners become one: ***"Wherefore they are no more twain, but one flesh" (Matthew 19:6a).*** That being said, if you divorce your spouse, you will be taking them with you as you walk out the door. Your spouse will be in the back of your mind; you will not be able to hide even one single action. The Bible says in ***Numbers 32:23b, "Be sure your sin will find you out."*** Memories are forever good and bad. As much as you would like to forget all the things that happened or that were said leading to the final split, not one word or episode can be taken back. Each word or action becomes a memory to someone.

Children see and hear things that they don't understand. When their parents are yelling, screaming, and fighting over their personal life, somehow those children think that all the endless turmoil is their fault. Believe it or not, they are burdened with those memories into adulthood and perhaps for a lifetime.

Truly I believe that if those considering divorce knew the path of destruction they were deciding to take and if they could see the end results of their selfish decision, they would disregard the idea completely. I have to admit that as much as I did not want my marriage to end, all of my attempts to save it failed. Without airing all of the ugly details, immaturity played the biggest part in the devastating destruction of the lives of my family.

People who are willing to jump off the wall of marriage have no idea how high the wall is or how long it will take to hit bottom. They do not realize, or perhaps do not care, that when they jump, they will take away the structure and security of an entire family from that point on. The shattered pieces of the family may never be put back together again.

If by chance you think the divorce is not at all your fault, it being all your unscrupulous spouse's fault, think again. It is very hard to see your own part in the arguments or how a snooty attitude opened the door to an explosive situation that would later lead to the desire to get even with that monster you made a lifetime commitment with.

There are a few things worth mentioning before we go on. For example, I want to mention those thoughts of revenge you have right now. Come on, I know you have them because that is how we humans seem to want to deal with those who claimed to love us yet hurt us. We automatically want to hurt them right back—and hurt them worse if at all possible. However, I'll give it to you straight: revenge is not the answer. I know if we were sitting face to face right now, you would be asking me how I know revenge is not the proper solution to making you feel better. You see, I attended the school of the hardest knocks, and I tried revenge—not a good idea. I beg of you; do not go there.

If only I had known and applied the following verses from the Bible, things might have turned out differently. ***Romans 12:19-21: "Dearly beloved, avenge not yourselves, but rather give place unto wrath: for it is written, Vengeance is mine; I will repay, saith the Lord. Therefore if thine enemy hunger, feed him; if he thirst, give him drink: for in so doing thou shalt heap coals of fire on his head. Be not overcome of evil, but overcome evil with good."*** The advice in the above Scripture is really a command by God, *"...avenge not yourselves."*

I would never have taken my anger out on the lunches I fixed for my husband every day if I had known that vengeance was God's job. *"**Vengeance is mine; I will repay, saith the Lord.**"* Believe me, I paid a price for brutalizing my husband's food. Well, who knew that the plastic wrap left on a slice of cheese placed between two pieces of bread poked full of holes could rile a guy up like it did him. Or it may have been the smashed potato chips and the cans of soda I shook up before I neatly packed them in his lunch box that sent him over the edge. I'm not really sure. But I can tell you that my snooty actions did not make me feel better; however, they did escalate other problem areas in our marriage. My attempt at revenge had the same effect as adding fuel to a fire, and all the while our children were listening, watching, and wondering.

By the way, **"heap coals of fire on his head"** did not mean that as soon as my husband opened his lunch box, a load of red hot coals suddenly landed on his head. Our motivation should never be to do good to someone in order to bring more misery into their life than they brought into ours. Our being kind to our enemies allows God to handle the situation in a just manner. God would have justly handled my husband's ill-mannered ways, but when **I** took matters into **my** own hands, **my** way only escalated every detail of our failing marriage. Trying to get **my** own way was not the route to success. The solution would have been to trust God to work things out in His perfect way. Unfortunately, at this point in my life, I had no idea what it meant to trust God and neither did my husband.

I fully believe with all my heart that if I had known about God's cleansing Word, I could have avoided so many heartaches in my life and in the lives of my children. I don't know about you, but before becoming a child of God, I didn't even recognize that some of my actions or words were sins.

Suppose a person is not raised in a Christian environment (I know I wasn't and neither was my husband). We only know what we are taught, and if God's Word was not involved in our upbringing, then we are at a tremendous disadvantage. How can we be obedient children to God if we do not know who He is or what He expects of us?

I had always rejected anyone's trying to tell me anything about God. After all, I was a Catholic and thought the born again were cultish, so I wanted nothing to do with them. But... when my mother was on her death bed with no hope left for recovery, I was told to contact the family.

The notified family members began to arrive a few at a time, and we all gathered in a small room provided for us by the hospital. When my father's born again Christian cousin and wife arrived, one of my sisters came right out and said, "We don't want any religion, so just keep it to yourselves." They responded with an, "Okay," and did just that—until my sister was not around. Then the cousin asked me if I would mind if he went in and talked to my mother about the Lord.

I answered, "If she doesn't mind, neither do I." So when the cousin went in to visit with my mother, I went to find the hospital chapel. On my knees, now praying for my mother's sake, I asked God to do whatever was best for her. I was no longer focusing on my selfish losses, but on her pain and suffering. Oh, how I hoped He would hear me. All I knew about God was that He was in Heaven and could see and hear everything, but I hadn't seen or heard from Him yet...

My cousin was in the family waiting room when I came back from the chapel. He thanked me for letting him have that opportunity to speak to my mother; then he told me she had accepted the Lord as her personal Savior. I really had no idea what that meant, but when I went in to see her, I sensed something different about her.

It was difficult for her to communicate because she was on life support; however, that didn't keep her from trying. She tried telling me that she was going "Home," but because I did not really know what she was trying to say, I just agreed with her.

She could tell I was not catching on. She started pointing to the ceiling. "No, mom, we are on the top floor now. They are not going to move you." I could see she was getting frustrated, so I started playing the guessing game with her. When I finally got it out of her that Home was Heaven, I wanted to know how she knew that. She mouthed, "Because Jesus told me so."

When my mother went home to be with the Lord, I faced a tremendous loss. Years later after I had moved back to California, a Baptist preacher, the cousin of my ex-husband Humpty, came to our local church to preach a five-day revival. Humpty agreed to go to church with me for the last day of the revival, and it was like no other church service I had ever attended. That was the very first time I actually heard the plan of salvation.

I went to that same church the following Sunday to hear what the local preacher had to say. He was very interesting, so eventually I started attending regularly. It was a rare occasion if the plan of salvation was not given, and each time I heard that plan, I felt awful when I didn't respond.

The preacher would always say, "With heads bowed and eyes closed and nobody looking around, if you would like to accept Christ as your personal Savior, just raise your hand and put it right back down. I'd like to pray for you."

I waited months before I raised my hand for the first time, and even then it was a tremendous struggle. As my head was bowed deep in humiliation, I felt a tapping on my shoulder, which scared me half to death. I was very relieved when I realized it was only the hand of an usher and not the hand of God.

The usher wanted to know if I would like to go to the altar and be shown how I could know, for sure, that Heaven was my home. I said, "No, not today." Can you believe it? I said no, not knowing when I would draw my last breath, causing me to be cast into hell for eternity.

Then one day I found myself at the altar. I have no idea how I got there or why I went, but I was there. The preacher himself took the Bible and showed me Scripture, convincing me that what he was telling me was not something he had made up but truth from the Word of God.

He started with ***John 3:16***, where the Bible says, ***"For God so loved the world that he gave his only begotten Son, that whosoever believeth in him should not perish, but have everlasting life."*** That verse got me to thinking. Yes, I was skeptical—because how could I believe in God's Son when I didn't even know who God was. I mean, I knew there was a God in Heaven, but I had never seen Him or met Him personally or anything like that.

Then there was *John 3:17*, *"For God sent not his Son into the world to condemn the world; but that the world through him might be saved."* I began to realize that I was a "whosoever" and that I could be saved. But saved from what?

Romans 3:10-12, cleared that up for me, *"As it is written, There is none righteous, no, not one: There is none that understandeth, there is none that seeketh after God. They are all gone out of the way, they are together become unprofitable; there is none that doeth good, no, not one."*

I had to admit that I was not righteous and needed to be saved from my sin because *Romans 6:23a* says, *"For the wages of sin is death."* Because of my sin, I deserved to die and go to hell. The second part of *Romans 6:23*, went on to say, *"The gift of God is eternal life through Jesus Christ our Lord."*

When I finally understood that I was a condemned sinner and that I deserved to spend an eternity in hell permanently separated from God's love, I was ready to accept Jesus Christ as my Savior and thus the gift of eternal life that God so freely offered. I realized that Jesus, God's Son, had suffered and died for all my sins so that I would not have to spend an eternity in hell. *Romans 5:8* says, *"But God commendeth his love toward us, in that, while we were yet sinners, Christ died for us."*

But there was something I had to do: I had to confess that I was a sinner, just as the Bible says in *Romans 10:9* and *10*, *"That if thou shalt confess with thy mouth the Lord Jesus, and shalt believe in thine heart that God hath raised him from the dead, thou shalt be saved. For with the heart man believeth unto righteousness; and with the mouth confession is made unto salvation."* After all that, when the Preacher asked me if I would like to accepted Jesus Christ as my personal Savior, I said, "Yes." Praise the Lord! I accepted Jesus as my Savior.

I had no idea what to expect from that point, but it turns out that my decision it was the beginning of a new life for me.

Then through reading my Bible daily, my eyes were opened to so many sinful things that I had once considered acceptable. I still cringe at some of those memories. I began to see things in such a different way.

- **Questions to think about:**

1. Are you courteous to your spouse? Ask the Holy Spirit to point out your improper mannerisms so you can become more Christlike toward your spouse. List the things that the Holy Spirit points out to you and refer to them frequently. Old habits are hard to break.

_____
_____
_____
_____
_____
_____
_____
_____

2. Have you accepted Christ as your personal Savior?

Yes _____ No _____

If your answer was yes, write out your salvation testimony as a reminder that Jesus Christ paid the price for all your sins on the Cross at Calvary. If your answer was no, perhaps today is the day to make that decision. You can find a more in-depth explanation of God's plan of salvation in the back of this book.

_____
_____
_____
_____
_____
_____
_____
_____

- **Verses to memorize:**

    1. *1 Peter 3:1, "Likewise, ye wives, be in subjection to your own husbands; that, if any obey not the word, they also may without the word be won by the conversation of the wives."*

    2. *1 Peter 3:7, "Likewise, ye husbands, dwell with them according to knowledge, giving honour unto the wife, as unto the weaker vessel, and as being heirs together of the grace of life; that your prayers be not hindered."*

    3. *1 Corinthians 6:20, "For ye are bought with a price: therefore glorify God in your body, and in your spirit, which are God's."*

- **Passages to read:**

    1 Peter 3
    James 1

Chapter 4

All the Kings Horses and All the Kings Men...

Some married couples think that their divorce is a private matter and that their decision to end their marriage is nobody's business but theirs. I personally do not agree. After all, the marriage vows were not a private matter; they were made before those who attended the wedding. A divorce involves countless people, starting with the children, then proceeding to the other family members of the husband and wife. The rippling effects of a divorce reach out as far as the divorcing couple's friends and their friends' families, not to mention co-workers. I am not exaggerating in the least. Keep in mind that there is no peaceful divorce and a fresh start does not exist.

Because marriage is a target at which Satan is constantly aiming, we must stay focused on the Word of God and the guidance that the Bible has to offer, which surprisingly enough is free. All we have to do is read. I am fully persuaded that if we took the Word of God seriously and followed it in our homes, the family unit could be brought back to the way God meant for it to be. *"Be not wise in thine own eyes: fear the LORD, and depart from evil" (Proverbs 3:7).* While divorce may seem wise in our own eyes, we must trust the Lord to help us work through our difficulties because running away is not the answer to our problems. If we want to have a happy marriage, we cannot disregard the principles and the instructions the Word of God so freely offers to us. ***Proverbs 14:12, "There is a way which seemeth right unto a man, but the end thereof are the ways of death."***

If you are considering divorce, please take the time to look carefully at what you and your household will suffer as a result of that dreadful decision. It's wedding day. The newlyweds are showered with gifts given by their family and friends from both sides. Those gifts were given to them as a couple, to be shared with each other as they start their new life together, not given to them as individuals. Now of course that was just a start, and as time goes on the couple buys other things: furniture, linens, dishes, and more. Every purchase required time, thought, and hard-earned money.

Pretty soon the typical couple adds a new member to the family, causing them to look for a bigger car. As the family continues to grow, the couple makes the decision to purchase their first home. A few more years down the road, everyday life begins to grow very hectic because of unexpected financial burdens that might require overtime or the need for additional part-time employment. With less time for each other, the couple's relationship begins to suffer. The arguments and disagreements are more frequent; the blaming of each other begins and will become more damaging as time goes by. Then either one or both will start thinking, "I can't take this anymore." That thought graduates into *I don't have to put up with this anymore*, and the seed of divorce begins to grow.

Now take a look at this picture from the children's point of view. They have heard all the arguments day after day, week after week, and uncertainty has moved into their minds and hearts. No matter their age, they are just children who are without a voice concerning the decisions made by their parents—decisions that will devastate them and alter their future.

When the decision of divorce has been declared and one of their parents walks out of the house and moves elsewhere, the security of that home leaves also. As time goes on, insecurity and uncertainty fill the children's minds and hearts (even if those children are adults themselves). Sooner or later the children begin to believe that what is happening is their fault, so they take on a feeling of guilt.

The real battle comes next, and once again the children are not consulted. Who gets the car, the house, the furniture? The final question is who gets custody of the children and who gets visitation rights. Once those decisions have been made, unwanted chaos is forced into the daily lives of the children. They either don't get to see the other parent at all, or visitation is sporadic. Visitation may be once a week, every other weekend, or once a month—you get the picture. In some cases, the parents use the children as pawns in a dangerous game of revenge, as leverage to influence the court system, or as bargaining chips with their spouse in order to gain what they want. Bottom line, the children know when they are being used.

By this time, the children are so frustrated, confused, and angry that they begin to act out. In their minds they don't fit in anymore, but that is not the worst of the problems. Just wait until their mom or their dad makes yet another devastating decision for them by bringing in an interloper. An *interloper* is a person who is not wanted or welcome, and when this takes place, resentment jumps right to the top of list, superseding insecurity, uncertainty, guilt, and anger.

The children see that the interloper is taking time and attention away from them, and their anger increases to bitterness. Some children will become clinging whiners, and others may isolate themselves. Introducing a new love interest into an already fragmented family puts the children in a vulnerable position, but the word *vulnerable* doesn't fully describe the dreadful position the selfish decision of divorce puts them in. *Vulnerable* means "susceptible, weak, defenseless, helpless, exposed and open to, in danger, and at risk." If you think divorce would not place your children in a vulnerable position, think again. So many times the live-in lover or new spouse will not treat your children with the love you expected them to. Keep in mind that no child—male or female—is safe from a potential child molester that you might unsuspectingly bring into your home.

Children are not allowed to argue with their siblings or friends, but the parents will engage in arguing regularly in front of their children without having to apologize or suffering any apparent type of punishment. The parents will often stomp off, slamming doors behind them or even hopping in the car, squealing the tires as they recklessly back out of the driveway. This behavior is just a temper tantrum, something the children are not allowed to indulge in. The double standard that parents demonstrate is not only frustrating but also very confusing to the children. The training of your children takes place every minute of every day, and what they see and hear cannot be erased from their minds. Some children may choose to put hurtful experiences in the back of their minds, but other children will see and hear those hurtful events over and over again for the rest of their lives, and both types of memories will affect their future in not only picking a spouse but also raising their children.

Believe it or not, in the home the parents are teaching their children how to become husbands, wives, and parents. I am not making excuses for my mistakes and weaknesses, but I would have loved to have a Godly example of how a marriage should be. The Bible says in **Proverbs 22:6, "Train up a child in the way he should go: and when he is old, he will not depart from it."** The training that you give your children—good or bad—will remain a part of their lives forever.

Divorce affects the family in the following ways:

- Spiritually

2 Corinthians 6:14, "Be ye not unequally yoked together with unbelievers: for what fellowship hath righteousness

with unrighteousness? And what communion hath light with darkness?"

When a farmer picks a pair of oxen, he wants them to be as close to the same height, length, and weight as possible so that when the oxen are yoked together and set to plowing a field, their steps will be very close to the same. Closely matched oxen will both be pulling the same weight at the same time, and the plowing will go smoothly and without struggle. When one ox is bigger than the other, the wooden frame they are yoked together with will begin to rub and become irritating, allowing open wounds to develop and making it impossible for them to plow effectively. Not one but both oxen will receive wounds.

The comparison the Bible is making here is that Jesus is the light and the world is darkness; unbelievers cannot comprehend the things of God, nor can they understand the thinking of a believer. *John 8:12 says, "... I am the light of the world: he that followeth me shall not walk in darkness, but shall have the light of life."* I have known married couples that were unequally yoked. The struggle is always there: husbands and wives going in opposite directions and constantly arguing because they do not have the same purpose in life, one wanting to live the worldly ways and the other wanting to live for the Lord Jesus.

If others are watching a Christian couple going through a divorce, they may use that failed marriage to excuse their choice to marry an unbeliever. However, the spiritual tug of war is very, very fierce in an unequally yoked marriage. Just imagine living like that your entire married life.

A wife who decides to trust Christ and is already married to an unbeliever can take courage from *1 Peter 3:1* and *2, "Likewise, ye wives, be in subjection to your own husbands; that, if any obey not the word, they also may without the word be won by the conversation of the wives; While they behold your chaste conversation coupled with fear."* Chaste means "pure, faithful, moral, virtuous, and honorable." The word *conversation* in the Bible does not just mean talking; it also involves our behavior. Remember actions speak louder than words, so your behavior will do the talking for you. *Fear* in this Scripture means respect, not only for your husband but also for God. Simply put, live consistently every day in such a way that your husband knows that you love and respect him. Proper actions and reactions can cause him to see his need for Christ as his Savior. Trust the Word of God. I have personally witnessed God work through the Godly life of a wife on more than one occasion.

When any married couple gets a divorce, especially if they are Christians, it's as though their actions grant permission for others to do the same. Others are watching us and most of the time without our knowledge. They see us, they hear us, and they depend on us to live like Christ. If you deceive yourself into thinking that your divorce is justified, you will also be deceiving others. If you lie to yourself, you are lying to others, and that includes those you love. Divorce truly is like an epidemic. Just the word *divorce* plants the seed of discontent and causes the spectators to think that the person who has just divorced has gained freedom from all responsibilities and accountability. The divorced one thinks he has the opportunity for a fresh start, but that is definitely not true since he cannot escape the obligations of the failed marriage. What really has happened is that he has further complicated his life. The suggestion of divorce sets the next unhappy couple's divorce in motion with if-they-can-do-it-so-can-I thinking.

As Christians, we are to follow what God's written Word says. I confess that it is very difficult to follow God's Word if your thoughts are only on your current circumstances and you're trying to work things out for yourself. Divorce is never part of God's perfect plan. He never meant for us to work things out our way. ***Isaiah 53:6a, "All we like sheep have gone astray; we have turned everyone to his own way."*** He has the perfect solution to every one of our circumstances already worked out for us. ***Proverbs 3:6, "In all thy ways*** *acknowledge him, and he shall direct thy paths."* However, pride will keep you from following God's perfect plan. ***Proverbs 16:18, "Pride goeth before destruction, and an haughty spirit before a fall."***

It is very hard to be kind to someone who is not being kind to you. Nevertheless, Christians are expected to continue to be nice to those who say and do mean and cruel things to them even when it is done on purpose. The Bible says in ***Ephesians 4:32, "And be ye kind one to another, tenderhearted, forgiving one another, even as God for Christ's sake hath forgiven you."***

With pride in the way, it is virtually impossible for a Christian to follow God's Word, but ***Philippians 4:13*** says, *"I can do all things through Christ which strengtheneth me."* The unkindness of a spouse is never a reason for ending a marriage. Divorce does not have to be the answer. You can still be kind even when it seems impossible. ***Matthew 19:26b, "With God all things are possible."***

We all want the security of knowing that we are loved by those we love. As long as daily life is going our way, that feeling of love is there. But when our loved ones are opposed to our plans or desires that is when the problems begin. True love is not required to fulfill every desire and dream. Some desires are selfish and hurtful to the marriage. Well, who said that it is mandatory that we should get our way every single time in order to be assured of being loved? If our spouse does not meet our every demand, we should not feel threatened that we are no longer loved.

In the summer of 1973, when my youngest son was scarcely three years old, he and his two older brothers (ages five and seven) were taking a bath together when I noticed a new bar of soap had been cut into three pieces. Believe me, I was caught off guard when the three year old said he had cut the soap up. I asked him what he had used to cut the soap with, and he said, "A knife." When I asked him why he cut the soap, he responded,

"Just in case three men wanted to take a bath together, they would all have some."

Once the boys were out of the bath, I asked the little confessor to show me the knife that he had used. I watched as he dragged a chair over to the kitchen counter, climbed up onto the chair, then onto the counter. He opened the top drawer, identifying his cutting tool (the biggest knife I had). He took the mammoth knife out of the drawer, and with it still clutched in his hand, he started to climb down onto the chair. I quickly intervened, taking the knife from him but allowing him to finish climbing down. He carefully put the chair back and looked very pleased with himself. It dawned on me right then and there that I had underestimated this child.

My young son had made a dangerous and potentially deadly decision because he had seen me use that knife to cut things up, and it looked like the perfect solution to his obvious problem. The truth is that he could have killed himself if he had fallen with the knife in his hand. ***Proverbs 14:12, "There is a way which seemeth right unto a man, but the end thereof are the ways of death."*** Divorce is a dangerous and potentially deadly decision. Perhaps you have watched someone else go through a divorce seemingly unscathed. Do not be deceived. Divorce does not solve problems, though you may not recognize the problems from your vantage point.

The answer to your marital problems is not found in your own understanding but in God's Word and the counsel of wise men. ***Proverbs 3:5, "Trust in the LORD with all thine heart; and lean not unto thine own understanding."*** My son did not seek advice; he simply took matters into his own hands. We know only what we are taught. We learn by watching, listening, and following wise men. ***Proverbs 11:14, "Where no counsel is, the people fall: but in the multitude of counsellors there is safety."*** A wise counselor knows Christ as his Savior and follows the precepts of the Bible. Because God originated marriage and the family, He has all the answers for happiness in our home.

- Financially

Proverbs 5:10, "Lest strangers be filled with thy wealth; and thy labours be in the house of a stranger." Property or money should never be the focal point in a marriage relationship. However, once the decision of divorce has been made, money often comes to the forefront. ***1 Timothy 6:10, "For the love of money is the root of all evil: which while some coveted after, they have erred from the faith, and pierced themselves through with many sorrows."***
Often in the courtroom, the true evil of the heart is exposed. The shocking truth is, divorcing parents sometimes love their money more than they love their children. When money is involved, this is where the nasty fight begins: clawing, biting, scratching, and poking out eyes. Both sides of the divorce will be forced to fight over everything from bank accounts to the family dog. While the debate rages on, the children are fearfully wondering, "Where do I fit in this picture? Will I even get to keep my dog?"
Have you ever considered all the financial setbacks divorce causes? Think about it: where there was once one household to financially care for, now there are two. Whether there were two incomes or just one, these monies will now be greatly reduced. Everything will double: not only travel expenses, child care, health insurance, car insurance, and a second residence, but also dishes, pots and pans, linens, furniture. The list is endless. You might be thinking, "That would be easy. Everything is half mine, I will take what is mine with me when I go." I have always found it very difficult to divide a refrigerator or a stove in half.
A wife may have to go to work, possibly for the first time, and someone else will raise the children. Who knows what your children will be taught or what they will be allowed to get away with. Eating out becomes more common because time has been greatly reduced. Take note that less time in general

means less time spent with the children, and then there could be the dreaded weekend trips to the laundromat for one of you.

Now if these thoughts aren't enough to make you reconsider divorcing, perhaps this will....

Sooner or later, guilt will enter the picture. The guilt causes the children to be caught up in a vicious circle of bigger gifts and more expensive vacations, not to mention giving in to your children's latest demands and enabling your children to become skilled at manipulation. Children become proficient at pitting one parent against the other in order to get their way.

When the judge's gavel falls with the final decision concerning your divorce, you might think that that would be the end of it. Think again. There is no end to a divorce. When there is a judgment of alimony or child support, the person required to pay the support no longer has control over how that money will be spent. Watching your money going for something other than for your children can be a continuing source of irritation and frustration. When the court system is involved in your finances, you will see the results of not heeding God's warning, **Proverbs 5:10a, "Lest strangers be filled with thy wealth...."**

- Emotionally

Proverbs 14:26, "In the fear of the LORD is strong confidence: and his children shall have a place of refuge." The seeds of divorce were planted early in my married life because of worldly decisions and biblical illiteracy. My husband's and my decisions were based on emotions, and I can tell you those seeds later blossomed into a divorce that yielded irreversible damage. Two of our four children have experienced divorce in their own marriages. Watching my children suffer the consequences of careless decisions was overwhelming, but witnessing my precious grandchildren suffer for those same decisions is absolutely devastating.

When a new step-parent or a live-in partner enters the home, potential threats often arise. In most cases, the interloper will not treat your children the way you expect them to, and the bad news is...you will not treat the interloper's children the way you treat your own. Favoritism is a gigantic problem amongst step-children. Children will feel left out when there are graduations, weddings, and vacations where they are not invited to come along because the new family is taking their place. A blended family rarely runs smoothly, but look out if a new baby enters into the picture.

I have listened to many ladies tell me of their horrifying life experiences as a result of coming from a divorced family. One marvelous young lady has spent years thinking that it was her fault that her parents divorced. As a result, she keeps to herself because she is ashamed, thinking that she was the cause of her parents' splitting up. Guilt still has her in bondage. Another darling young lady was molested for years by her step-father; as a result, she has attempted suicide more than once. Another fabulous older lady confessed that in her search for a lasting, loving relationship, she gave birth to five children, all of whom have different fathers. She is still looking for a marriage that will provide spiritual, financial, and emotional security. Hope remains for you if your life has been devastated by the effects of divorce. The Bible says in ***Psalm 68:6: "God setteth the solitary in families: he bringeth out those which are bound with chains: but the rebellious dwell in a dry land."***

• Questions to think about:

1. What consequences of your actions could directly affect your family? Be sure to also include those that I may not have mentioned in this chapter.

_____
_____
_____
_____
_____
_____
_____
_____

2. Have you considered seeking counseling from a pastor? Yes_____ No_____

List your reasons as to why or why not.

_____
_____
_____
_____
_____
_____
_____
_____
_____

- **Verses to memorize:**

    1. *Proverbs 3:5, "Trust in the Lord with all thine heart; and lean not unto thine own understanding."*

    2. *Philippians 4:13, "I can do all things through Christ which strengtheneth me."*

    3. *Amos 3:3, "Can two walk together, except they be agreed?"*

- **Passages to read:**

    Psalm 121
    Proverbs 4

Chapter 5

Couldn't Put Humpty Together Again...

I had often said, "Thanks, but no thanks" to the religious, door-knocking crowd. I shut the door in their faces before they had a chance to say the word *salvation*. Never mind giving them the opportunity to tell me how God's perfect plan could change everything if I would let it. No, salvation cannot erase your past, but it can change your future.

The Encarta Dictionary defines *salvation* as "1. The saving of somebody or something from harm, destruction, difficulty, or failure 2. In the Christian religion, deliverance from sin or the consequences of sin through Jesus Christ's death on the cross 3. Deliverance, rescue, recovery, and escape." Salvation was what I needed, but I closed the door so many times before I found out how to obtain it. Little did I know that without salvation, my final destination was hell for eternity.

I remember explaining salvation to one of my young grandsons during breakfast one morning. I do not remember just what put us on the subject, but he asked what salvation meant. When I asked him if he had ever sinned, he ashamedly admitted that he sinned lots of times. When I asked him if he had ever sinned against God, his eyes began to water as he hung his head and admitted that he had sinned against God too.

That is when I quoted *John 3:16: "For God so loved the world that he gave his only begotten Son, that whosoever believeth in him should not perish, but have everlasting life."* He wanted to know what everlasting life meant, so I explained that it meant "to live forever."

I also quoted *John 3:3b*, where Jesus said, *"Except a man be born again, he cannot see the kingdom of God,"* and I went on to tell my grandson that the kingdom of God is heaven.

"Born again. What's born again?" he asked. Well, how does one explain born again? YIKES! This kid was full of questions. With the Bible at my fingertips, I was able to give him an answer to every question he had.

My first question to him was, "Were you born to your mother?"

His answer to me was simply, "Yes."

With that settled, I recited *John 3:6, "That which is born of the flesh is flesh; and that which is born of the Spirit is spirit."* I then pointed to his arm and said, "This is the flesh, so you have been born of the flesh already, but now you need to be born of the Spirit in order to become a Christian."

His next question was, "But how do I do that?"

So I went to *Romans 6:23* because it was imperative that he know that *"...the wages of sin is death; but the gift of God is eternal life through Jesus Christ our Lord."* I told him that Christ was the only begotten Son of God and that Christ was innocent because He had never sinned.

However, because the wages of sin is death and *"...all have sinned, and come short of the glory of God" (Romans 3:23)*, we all deserve to die and go to hell forever.

He got a worried look on his face, but I assured him that God knows we are all sinners and because sin cannot enter into heaven, anyone who is willing to accept Christ's death as payment for their sin would never die but have everlasting life with Him in heaven.

Then my grandson wanted to know about the gift and how he could get the gift God had for him. I told him the gift is Jesus Christ and that by accepting Christ as his personal Savior, his sins would be fully paid for and he would be spiritually born into the family of God.

That is when I asked him if he would like to accept Christ as his personal Savior and he said, "Yes, Grandma."

Fabulous, this conversation was going great, but I had to be sure he fully understood that God is the one and only God and that Christ is the only Savior. So I asked him if he thought God had created the entire world and everything in it.

He answered, "Of course, I know that."

So then I asked him if he thought God the Father, God the Son, and God the Holy Spirit were all the same person, to which he replied, "Yes, I believe that too."

The next question I had for him was, "Do you believe that Christ died, that He was buried, that He rose again on the third day, and that He still lives today and is sitting at the right hand of God the Father in Heaven right now?

His answer was, "Yes, Grandma I believe that too."

I told him that all he had to do now was to confess out loud that he was a sinner and ask Christ to forgive him of his sins and to be his very own personal Savior.

I showed him what the Bible says in **Romans 10:9** and **10**, *"That if thou shalt confess with thy mouth the Lord Jesus, and shalt believe in thine heart that God hath raised him from the dead, thou shalt be saved. For with the heart man believeth unto righteousness; and with the mouth confession is made unto salvation."*

I followed those verses up with **Romans 10:13,** *"For whosoever shall call upon the name of the Lord shall be saved."*

Then I showed him *John 14:6*, where Jesus said, *"I am the way, the truth, and the life: no man cometh unto the Father, but by me."*

It truly was the sweetest acceptance of Christ I have ever witnessed. After he had confessed and accepted Christ, he raised his head from praying and, with tears of regret streaming down his face, managed to say, "But I didn't want Him to have to die because of me."

Just saying you are a Christian does not make you a Christian, neither does the fact that you grew up in a Christian home. Even going to church nine months before you were born doesn't make you a Christian. Unless you have accepted Christ as your personal Savior, you are just one heartbeat away from spending an eternity in hell.

I showed my grandson how he could rest assured that he could never lose his salvation or his place in Heaven with a promise he could cling to for eternity. These are the words of Jesus found in *John 10:28-30: "And I give unto them eternal life; and they shall never perish, neither shall any man pluck them out of my hand. My Father, which gave them me, is greater than all; and no man is able to pluck them out of my Father's hand. I and my Father are one."*

It is no secret that the Word of God changes the lives of those who belong to Him.

From the beginning of time, sin has been the separating factor between mankind and God. Sin causes division in a marriage as well. The only way to close that gap is to acknowledge, confess, and turn from the sins that find their way to the forefront of our everyday life.

Years after my husband and I were divorced and after we had remarried, I asked him how he viewed the results of divorce. This is what he said, "A divorce, first of all, is bad for the immediate family, the wife, and the kids. It would be bad enough if the negative effects stopped right there. But they don't stop there. All of your friends and relatives take sides and give opinions. Some will call you crazy; some will agree with you, but everyone on both sides of both families will be affected. The kids are always in the middle. Divided loyalties. Anger toward the one who left. Anger toward the parents' new friends ('if he or she was not around, maybe things would get back to normal'). No child should ever have to go through a divorce, and no parent should ever have to miss the wonderful experience of watching a child grow up and start his own family."

We did not divorce right away. Oh, no. That would have been way too easy and civilized. No, no, there was the yelling, screaming, and daily fighting, the throwing of things, the slamming of doors, and the squealing of tires as one of us drove off in a childish huff while our frightened babies stood watching it all unfold through their tear-filled eyes, wondering what would happen next.

Integrity is not living a "Godly" life on the outside while living a sinful life on the inside. Integrity is proven by your actions and your convictions from the inside out. In other words, it's how you deal with life's situations no matter what the circumstances are. Then and only then will others be convinced that you are a person of integrity. **Proverbs 20:7** says, ***"The just man walketh in his integrity: his children are blessed after him."***

I can tell you firsthand, there are no blessings involved in **divorce**—financially or otherwise. To keep things simple, I looked the word *integrity* up in the *Webster's Elementary Dictionary for Boys and Girls*. It means, "1.The condition or quality of being complete 2. Soundness; purity and honesty, as in a man of integrity." *Integrity* embodies the qualities needed to avoid divorce. *Integrity* is the total opposite of infidelity. In speaking with others, I have found that infidelity and finances are the major issues in the breakdown of a marriage.

If you are guilty of dishonorable and immoral behavior, it's not too late; pick up your Bible and start reading. You will find all the wisdom, knowledge, and understanding you need in the infallible Word of God. The Bible can show you not only how to acquire integrity for yourself through salvation but also how to save your marriage. From the beginning of time, sin has been the separating factor between mankind and God. The only way to close that gap is to acknowledge, confess, and turn from the sins that find their way to the forefront of our everyday life.

The Bible tells us that if we acknowledge God in all our ways, *"...he shall direct thy paths,"* as stated in **Proverbs 3:6b**. But know this, God's instructions and directions on how to achieve integrity will take action and courage on your part before they can become a reality in your life. I personally have found the book of Proverbs to be an invaluable and incalculable source of information. It is God's instruction book that teaches us how to avoid snares and pitfalls that Satan lays out for us in such tempting ways. The Bible says in **Proverbs 22:3, "A prudent man foreseeth the evil, and hideth himself: but the simple pass on, and are punished."** The word *prudent* means "sensible, wise, careful, and far-sighted." **Numbers 32:23, "But if ye will not do so, behold, ye have sinned against the LORD: and be sure your sin will find you out."**

The Bible tells us how to handle each and every situation that comes our way. Yes, we will struggle with the understanding of it at first, but the more we read, the more we will become acquainted with where to look for the answers that will give us the guidance we need. The truth of the Word of God has the power to change our lives.

It is very difficult, if not impossible, to have a close relationship with anyone without trust and honesty, which love is based upon. *Amos 3:3* says, *"Can two walk together, except they be agreed?"* Unless you are in agreement with God and His Word, your relationship with Him will not be close. When a husband and wife both choose to agree with the Word of God, they will find themselves agreeing with each other. Their common goal to please God causes them to draw closer to each other day by day.

Do you check with God and His plan for your life, or are you like I was, blindly following your deceitful heart to your own hurt? God is the only One Who can know your heart, and He knows it before you do because He has said, *"I the LORD search the heart" (Jeremiah 17:10a).* This is the reason we are instructed to *"Trust in the LORD with all thine heart..." (Proverbs 3:5a).* Rather than following our heart, we need to be grounded in the Word of God as we are seeking His will for our life.

Joshua 1:8 shows us that meditating on God's Word will put us on the path to success. *"This book of the law shall not depart out of thy mouth; but thou shalt meditate therein day and night, that thou mayest observe to do according to all that is written therein: for then thou shalt make thy way prosperous, and then thou shalt have good success."*

Have you ever noticed that many times we do not want to get out of our comfort zone? We do not want to follow the promptings of the Holy Spirit out of fear of the unknown or simply because that was not the way we were taught? Do you even recognize the promptings of the Holy Spirit? If so, are you willing to see what God can do with your submissive heart? ***James 4:7*** says, *"Submit yourselves therefore to God. Resist the devil, and he will flee from you."* And ***James 4:8a*** says that if you, *"Draw nigh to God... he will draw nigh to you."*

Some great and positive benefits come along with the word submit. By submitting yourself to God, you will not only get to know Him better, but as a result, you will also establish a closer relationship with Him. Submitting yourself to God gives you the opportunity to get to know who you are, enabling you to establish right relationships both with God and others.

Having a close relationship with God does not mean the Devil will automatically flee from you. You must resist the Devil through the power of God's Word. The Bible says that if you acknowledge God in all your ways, *"he shall direct thy paths,"* as stated in ***Proverbs 3:6b***. But remember, God's instructions and directions on how to achieve integrity will take action and courage on your part before integrity can become a reality in your life.

The book of Proverbs is God's instruction book that teaches us how to avoid snares and pitfalls that Satan lays out for us in such tempting and subtle ways. One example of the wisdom and instruction found in this book of the Bible is ***Proverbs 22:3***, *"A prudent man foreseeth the evil, and hideth himself: but the*

simple pass on, and are punished." The word *prudent* means "sensible, wise, careful, and far-sighted."

If we refuse to submit to the wisdom and instruction found in God's Word, we will not be prosperous and successful but will instead pay the penalty for our rebellion. **Numbers 32:23** says, ***"But if ye will not do so, behold, ye have sinned against the LORD: and be sure your sin will find you out."*** I would rather be successful by following God's Word than destroyed by following my own deceitful heart. Isn't it wonderful that God has given us a formula for prosperity and success in the Bible!

- **Questions to think about:**

1. How successful and prosperous do you want to be? How does God define success? (Joshua 1:8, Proverbs 3:5-7) In your own words, write down what these Scriptures teach us about God's view of success.

   _____
   _____
   _____
   _____
   _____
   _____

2. How close is your walk with God? List at least three things that you know the Holy Spirit is prompting you to change in your life.

   _____
   _____
   _____
   _____
   _____
   _____

3. Are you reading God's Word daily?

   Yes _____ No_____

   _____
   _____
   _____
   _____
   _____

- **Verses to memorize:**

    1. *Galatians 6:7-9, "Be not deceived; God is not mocked: for whatsoever a man soweth, that shall he also reap. For he that soweth to his flesh shall of the flesh reap corruption; but he that soweth to the Spirit shall of the Spirit reap life everlasting. And let us not be weary in well doing: for in due season we shall reap, if we faint not.*

    2. *Proverbs 30:5 "Every word of God is pure: he is a shield unto them that put their trust in him."*

- **Passages to read:**

    Galatians 5
    Proverbs 22

Chapter 6

But God Can...

Disappointment and anger gave way to bitterness that took me down the path of deep depression. I don't think I will ever be able to describe how heartsick I was when my marriage went from "I love you," to the first time I heard, "I don't want to be married anymore." After five short years of marriage, with two small children and a third on the way.

Anger entered in my life when I noticed unsettling changes taking place. Sometimes my husband didn't come home right after work because he was "talking" with the guys in the parking lot. In reality, he was drinking with the guys. That didn't happen very often at first. However, *"Wine is a mocker, strong drink is raging: and whosoever is deceived thereby is not wise" (Proverbs 20:1).*

Resentment took over when my husband's drinking and staying out late became a regular routine. Then when I suspected drugs and women had entered the picture, I was totally infuriated. Now I am not saying I was the perfect wife and let all those things go unchallenged. No, that was not the case. I was waiting for him when that husband of mine came through the door. Just like the perfect nagging wife, I started in with the questions and accusations. After listening to all the lies and denials, I was even more outraged as he insulted my intelligence. Because my pride had entered the picture, this was definitely not the right time or approach to discuss such matters. That was for sure. *"A soft answer turneth away wrath: but grievous words stir up anger" (Proverbs 15:1).*

Since I did not understand the part about keeping my voice calm, those angry words I spoke in response only escalated until they created an even bigger barrier between us called bitterness. If I had only known that truth found in God's Word, it might have been the saving grace of my marriage.

Although my husband's actions were a violation of our marriage vows and clearly against the teaching of God's Word, my response was neither loving nor Christlike. Neither of us were Christians at the time. The Bible says in *Proverbs 13:10, "Only by pride cometh contention: but with the well advised is wisdom."* When there is contention in a marriage, the contention is always rooted in pride. Just know that contention is only the beginning of the breakdown in a marriage. If not put in check, pride will destroy your marriage and any other relationships you have. *Proverbs 16:18, "Pride goeth before destruction, and an haughty spirit before a fall."*

After our third son was born, I had no idea how I was going to pay the bills because of the instability in our marriage. In order to protect myself, I felt I had no choice but to get a job. That is when I started smoking cigarettes, thinking that would calm my nerves. Both of my parents smoked, so it just seemed natural to me to turn to cigarettes. I can tell you that smoking was definitely not the answer. The journey to quit that expensive, filthy habit was an eighteen-year struggle. I don't recommend anyone falling into the trap of dependence on cigarettes.

In 1972 our entire family moved to Arizona, but not a single thing changed. My husband and I were still on the outs most of the time. We simply did not agree on very many things and argued about everything. Our arguing caused great turmoil and insecurity in the lives of our children. A lack of trust causes extensive damage to any marriage and to the entire family.

Because I was sick and tired of my life and didn't know how to change it, I didn't want to face another day. Anxiety and confusion now ruled my everyday life, causing me to make one bad decision after another. Up to this point, I had never experienced anything that affected my health so severely. I faced loss of appetite, a racing heart, insomnia, and exhaustion. That is certainly a terrifying place to be with three children to take care of.

Not knowing exactly what was wrong, I went to the doctor and was introduced to anti-depressant drugs. Doctors typically prescribe drugs as a quick fix to manage a deeper problem. The long and the short of this part of my life was that before I knew it, I was hooked on those drugs. The mildest form of anti-depressants soon gave way to the strongest on the market, and before long, even the strongest medicine was not enough to calm the nervousness of my out-of-control life. The truth was, I was trying to run from reality, which of course could not be accomplished. No one can escape reality.

When I realized that these pills were not the answer, I made up my mind to stop taking them, which was not an easy task. The struggle was so difficult, causing me not to be the easiest person to live with. Determination and staying focused on my job and family helped me to get through that misery. Even though I did not realize it at the time, God was working in my life to help me face my daily battles. He was seeking me even though I wasn't seeking Him. He continued to send people to my door with the message of salvation, but I sent them away.

In March of 1974, my husband hitch-hiked to California and got his old job back. In spite of all of the unsavory details that had been added to our already unstable marriage, the boys and I moved back to California to join him in June. But in 1975, my youngest son and I returned to Arizona in order for me to take advantage of the opportunity to attend cosmetology school, where my sister was the primary instructor, while the two older boys chose to stay with their dad in California. My son and I would be staying with my sister and her family. They had a little boy about the same age as mine, so it seemed like the perfect set up. But soon I would have to get a job, and I rarely had time to spend with my son as it was. I decided to take him back to California to stay with my husband who had been temporarily laid off; thus, his father would have more time to spend with him than I did.

Although I thought my absence would make my husband's heart grow fonder, this did not prove to be the case. Before I had finished school, my husband informed me that he wanted me to sign the divorce papers so he could marry someone else. Knowing I did not have the power to change his mind, I signed.

The Bible really is the perfect marriage manual. Our human reasoning will lead us astray when our thoughts are not based on the truths found in the Word of God. At times I thought running away from the situation was the answer, but it wasn't. At other times I thought staying was the answer, but it wasn't either. The only answers are found in the Word of God. ***Proverbs 3:5-7, "Trust in the LORD with all thine heart; and lean not unto thine own understanding. In all thy ways acknowledge him, and he shall direct thy paths. Be not wise in thine own eyes: fear the LORD, and depart from evil."***

I thought that with the divorce final and behind us, things would begin to get better. But no...that did not happen. The situation went from bad to worse. Even when I called to check on my sons, I was "that woman on the phone." Well, honestly! At the age of only twenty-six, could my life have gotten any worse? Yes. It did. My now ex-husband's new wife thought I should disappear. For sure, she didn't want me to call or show my face when I had a rare weekend off to spend with my sons. The reality of my existence must have seemed to her like a threat to the security of their marriage. The fact that my sister was married to my ex-husband's brother made life even more awkward.

Even though I was going to school six hours a day, six days a week and managing a quaint dress shop in the evenings after school, I still continued to find myself in trouble because of making unwise choices. I had already met several men before my divorce was final. Although I was not serious with any of them, I was attracted to one in particular. He was so kind to me and always polite; I found both his personality and his gentlemanly behavior very refreshing. Occasionally we would meet at a restaurant and sit for hours, talking and enjoying each other's company. Wow! How in the world did all the women let this one get away? I couldn't believe it when he asked me to marry him. Little did I know that his pleasant facade would lead eventually to a life filled with apprehension and fear? Following my heart seemed to be the right thing to do but soon led me into dangerous territory. **Proverbs 28:26,** *"He that trusteth in his own heart is a fool: but whoso walketh wisely, he shall be delivered."*

Now don't think for one moment that I am the only one who has gone blindly to the altar as the result of false promises. I am not. Though I had known this man for approximately a year, in reality I knew nothing about him or his past. After the divorce papers from my previous marriage were signed, I introduced Prince Charming to my parents, my sisters, and my sons.

Although I was completely honest and open with him about my past, the same was not true for him. There were no family members to meet, nor were there any friends or co-workers for me to observe his interactions with. He told me he had never married and had no children. The lack of information should have been a warning of something more to come because I knew only what he told me and how he presented himself in my presence. **Proverbs 12:15** says, *"The way of a fool is right in his own eyes: but he that hearkeneth unto counsel is wise."* I certainly was not wise by any stretch of the imagination. I am not making any excuses here, but I was so caught up in his charm that I could only see and hear the fairytale words—*and they lived happily ever after.*

I never questioned the fact that I had never seen Prince Charming without his cowboy hat—until we went dancing on our first official date. Therefore, I was a little shocked that night when black streaks started streaming down both sides of his sweaty face just after our third time on the dance floor. I had no idea that he had dyed his own hair—what was left of it—to match the color of his pompadour toupee. Before I could figure out how to approach the delicate situation, the blunt, outspoken waitress asked him if he needed a rag to wipe the black streaks off his face. Well, it all just happened so fast! What an embarrassing situation it was for the three of us. So that cat was out of the bag.

Prince Charming had graying hair and was balding, which was no big deal to me. I have nothing against bald people or toupees for that matter. After all, I was still in school, hoping to pursue a career in the hair business. In any case, how was I to know what he was hiding under his cowboy hat? I wasn't zeroing in on his hair. Besides, from where I sat, that deception looked so real. I use the word *deception* because he was deliberately trying to hide his real self from me.

When the Prince and I got married in Laughlin, Nevada, with my mother and father standing up for us, I learned his true age for the first time as we were filling out our marriage licenses—a shocking eighteen years older than I! Okay, that startling revelation was still no game changer; I was in love after all.

Two months after we were married, Prince Charming and I were discussing why we hadn't received our marriage license. I told him I was not sure, but I acknowledged that it could be taking a little longer because they had to check to make sure my divorce was really final. It scared me half to death when he turned as white as a ghost and dropped straight to the floor. I didn't know what to think. I didn't know if I should call 911 or get a bucket of water. After he regained consciousness, I turned as white as a ghost when another cat flew out of the bag: Prince Charming admitted that he was still married to another woman.

Not only was he still married, but his wife and their four children were living somewhere in the New Jersey area. Wow! If I had known this interesting, revolting, and disheartening bit of information, it might have been a game changer for me—at least until he was divorced from her. How inconsiderate to keep such important information from me! At this point he told me he hadn't seen his family for fifteen years. (Wow! He had walked out on his family too!)

He said not to worry, that he had an attorney friend who could help us with a solution to this situation. The attorney made it sound so easy. He said that because my Prince Charming didn't have an address for his wife or know how to locate her, all he had to do was file a notice in the newspaper asking for a divorce, and if she didn't contest, six weeks later he would be a free man. Because I was so naïve, I thought the problem was solved. I found out later that the Prince and his attorney friend were drinking buddies, which shouldn't have surprised me because before we were married the Prince was a bartender on the weekends.

I was blindly trusting and very busy before we were married. In my innocence, I was totally unaware but found out later that when I met him, he had been living with a woman and six of their children. Well, how was I supposed to know? I didn't follow him around, and he always had plenty of time for me and was never in a hurry to leave. It was purely by accident that I found out this devastating information. Now the Prince was looking more like a frog.

Isn't love supposed to conquer all? As the years went by, more upsetting, even shocking events were revealed one by one about the man I had assumed was my Prince Charming.

Then there was the day I found out that he had a whole mouth full of false teeth! I found that out purely by mistake too. He went to great lengths to keep that information top secret. We hadn't been married long when I woke up in pain, wondering why the middle of my back was giving me so much grief. And what "to my surprise" did I find? A bottom set of dentures—that left a deep impression on me.

Well, yikes! That cat must have had kittens because another cat was out of the bag. How was I to know that his toupee was not the only thing that was removable? I wasn't zeroing in on his teeth. From where I sat, those teeth looked so real, and even though we were now married, he was still intentionally trying to hide his real self from me. This time I had a bit of fun just to see how he would go about keeping his top secret a top secret.

I kept quiet about my findings and watched him carefully make the bed as he searched frantically for his missing teeth. Nope, not there. He looked under and all around the bed. Nope, not there either. He continued his desperate search as nonchalantly as possible for several hours. He frantically rifled through trashcans, crawled on his hands and knees, and examined every nook and cranny, hoping to find his missing choppers.

I smiled inwardly, knowing why he never spoke a word to me during his search unless we were in separate rooms. Finally tired of waiting for him to tell me what he was doing, I asked, "Are you looking for these?" I pointed to his false teeth, now sitting in an obvious place on the counter, where I had placed them after pulling them out of my pocket. Looking sheepish and turning very pale, he nodded his head, picked them up, and disappeared to the bathroom for hours. So again he had been found out.

I wish I would have known the truth of **Proverbs 3:7** back then: ***"Be not wise in thine own eyes."*** Following God's wisdom would have saved me from many years of agonizing heartache. When the smoke screen of his deception began to clear, the truth came marching in unexpectedly in little bits and pieces. Sir Walter Scott wrote, "Oh, what a tangled web we weave, when first we practice to deceive!" Deceitfulness...oh, the lies and lengths people will go to in order to obtain their selfish goals. ***Jeremiah 17:9, "The heart is deceitful above all things, and desperately wicked: who can know it?"***

Looking back, I now see that there were so many warnings in the Bible that could have saved me from myself. I wish I would have known about the guidance of Scripture back then. If so, I could have avoided much of the heartache and sorrow in my life and in the lives of others by making wise, informed decisions. Unfortunately, because I was ignorant of the wisdom found in the Scriptures and so unwilling to even consider God's instructions, I continued to make foolish choices. *"They would none of my counsel: they despised all my reproof. Therefore shall they eat of the fruit of their own way, and be filled with their own devices." (Proverbs 1:30-31).*

It turns out he was in reality a paranoid schizophrenic who had self-medicated with alcohol for so long and to the point that he never appeared to be drunk. It was only when he tried to give up drinking that I found myself face to face with panic after a psychiatrist diagnosed the Prince as a paranoid schizophrenic right smack dab in front of me. Later that same psychiatrist cautioned me to always keep the Prince in front of me and instructed me to never trust the Prince but to always be aware of his behavior. He told me to never show my fear because the Prince was depending on my strength.

Now don't get me wrong. I was not then, nor am I now, the perfect one—not by a long shot. I found it possible to forgive and even forget many things, but murder and even an attempt on my life were not among them.

His paranoia kicked into high gear after a failed attempt at taking the prescribed medicine, which made him feel jittery and out of control. Consequently, he returned to drinking. As a result, he underwent horrific mood swings—from kind and loving to mean, scary and potentially dangerous. He trusted no one, including me. He tried to keep me from my family and friends, took the keys to my car, and moved us a far distance from anyone I knew. He even went as far as refusing to have a phone installed.

I remembered the time when my oldest son had chosen to live with his father in California and my two younger sons six and eight chose to live with me in Arizona. This particular day the two boys were at school, and the Prince was at work, so it left me home alone. I was lost in my thoughts while cleaning the house when suddenly I was attacked from behind. Strong hands were around my throat choking me. In a millisecond, I was struggling for my next breath and looking for a foot to stomp on, barely able to breathe, I went totally limp, and just before I completely passed out, I remember recognizing my assailant's boots. They belonged to my husband the Prince!

When I regained consciousness, I was alone and scared half to death. Knowing that from the Prince's past behavior, I would be putting myself in more danger if I stayed. I made up my mind to act like nothing out of the ordinary had taken place earlier in the day. That way when the Prince came home, everything would appear to be normal.

As part of my plan of escape, I held off on putting the laundry away. I neatly stacked each one of the boy's clothes in separate piles so it would be easier for me to put the clothes in bags at my first opportunity and hand the bags to the boys on their way to the car. I thank God to this day that those boys were obedient and followed all my instructions.

When the Prince arrived home, I was still very nervous, not knowing if my plan was going to work or not. I waited until he was showering, thinking that would be the best time to make our escape. We did escape, but just by the skin of our teeth.

I was shaking so badly that I could hardly put the car in reverse. When I backed out, I came face to face with the Prince. I quickly put the car in drive and pressed hard on the gas. Looking in the rearview minor, I saw the Prince running down the alley after us with only a towel around him...but we got away.

That all happened a few months after the Prince went off the deep end, becoming so paranoid that he felt it necessary to hold me and the two boys hostage in a motel room for three days at gun point. The boys never knew there was a gun involved, and I made it as fun as possible for them so they would not know the severity of the situation. The boys loved the Prince, and he loved them and would never in his right mind have hurt them. But he was not in his right mind. The Prince's agitation was the result of his taking the medicine the psychiatrist had prescribed to him instead of drinking alcohol, which put him at ease.

The boys went to live with their dad, and I went to northern California to stay with my oldest and youngest sisters for several months. Bad choices always bring consequences, and I kept making bad choices. I eventually moved back to Arizona. I hadn't pulled in to my parents' driveway more than an hour when a dozen roses arrived with a note saying, "I am glad you are back in town. Love, Prince." Well, you guessed it, Prince had gone back to drinking and was again like the guy I fell in love with, so we eventually got back together.

To make a long story short, Prince bought a bar, and one night the bar was robbed. Yes! I found myself looking down the barrel of a sawed-off shotgun. I gave up all the money without hesitation, but in all honesty, that event was not half as scary as living with a paranoid schizophrenic when he was having a bad day.

Eventually I gave the Prince an ultimatum that caused him to want to leave on his own. Much later, I had the marriage annulled. Even though I had moved back to California, I never saw him again but, I continued to live in silent fear for twenty-five years, thinking that he might show up in a paranoid state with murder on his mind.

Here was my downfall: God kept placing people in my life, and I kept rejecting them. I wanted nothing to do with the "born again" crowd; they were all hypocrites in my opinion.

Many years later, I have come to know that God has the answer to everything. In order to have a close relationship with anyone, you have to get to know them personally, and that also includes God. You may acknowledge that there is a God, that He is the Creator of Heaven, earth and all that is in between, and you may even know that God the Father, God the Son, and God the Holy Spirit are the three Who make up the Trinity. But if that is all you know about God, may I suggest to you that you don't know God any better than I knew the man I married. The only way you can get to know God is through His only begotten Son Jesus Christ.

We all make bad choices in life, and the consequences will always follow. The Word of God warns us in **Galatians 6:7,** *"Be not deceived; God is not mocked: for whatsoever a man soweth, that shall he also reap."*

God does not want us to live in fear. The Bible says in **2 Timothy 1:7,** *"For God hath not given us the spirit of fear; but of power, and of love, and of a sound mind."* When your life or the lives of your children are in danger, including mental or physical abuse, you should leave as soon as it is conceivably safe. Keep in mind that you cannot go where you would normally find love and safety. Go somewhere your abuser doesn't know. Just go!

There are shelters that know how to help in these types of circumstances, so find one in advance if time allows! Devise a plan, inform and instruct your children, and let them know the importance of their obedience and silence in the matter.

This is going to be a very difficult and emotional time for everyone. Even if your spouse apologizes, claims this will never happen again, and begs your forgiveness, this does not mean the pattern of abuse will end. Yes, you love your spouse and may even forgive him or her, but it will not change the situation. You will inadvertently be enabling them to continue in that abusive behavior, even empowering them because of your tolerance. God is still in control, and He knows what is going on in your life, so have courage in knowing that He will not give you more than you can deal with.

I firmly believe that **Romans 8:28** is true: *"...all things work together for good to them that love God, to them who are the called according to his purpose."* So if you have accepted Christ as your personal Savior, then you have the opportunity to claim this promise.

Do you love God? Are you sincerely willing to follow His commandments? Do you attend church regularly? Are you reading your Bible daily? Are you praying daily? Do you have an angry or unforgiving spirit? Does the way you live actually show that you love God, or are your words and actions contrary one to another?

Wait. Let me ask you this: "Have you ever accepted Christ as your personal Savior? If not, would you like to? The Bible says in *1 John 4:10, "Herein is love, not that we loved God, but that he loved us, and sent his Son to be the propitiation for our sins."* Verse 15 says, *"Whosoever shall confess that Jesus is the Son of God, God dwelleth in him, and he in God."* And then verses 18 and 19 say, *"There is no fear in love; but perfect love casteth out fear: because fear hath torment. He that feareth is not made perfect in love. We love him, because he first loved us."*

Nowhere does the Bible promise us that proverbial "bed of roses" or a life without trials or tribulations. However, God can take our trials and work them together for our good according to His purpose. Just as a cook uses different ingredients in a recipe, God chooses different events in our life to produce something good. Each ingredient may not taste good on its own, but put all together, the results are very delicious. Would you enjoy a teaspoon of baking soda? Of course not! Neither do we enjoy our individual trials. When we love God and are called according to His purpose, God can even take the foolish choices of our past and make a miracle out of our mess.

Each of us will have to endure some spiritual growing pains to make us more like Christ. *John 16:33b* says, *"In the world ye shall have tribulation: but be of good cheer; I have overcome the world."* There will be some undesirable situations in our life here on earth, but here is a shocking revelation: God expects us to glory in our trials. *"And not only so, but we glory in tribulations also: knowing that tribulation worketh patience; and patience, experience; and experience, hope: and hope maketh not ashamed; because the love of God is shed abroad in our hearts by the Holy Ghost which is given unto us" (Romans 5:3).*

Have I had trials and tribulations in my life? Yes—one right after another, to the point where I didn't know what to do, where to turn, or even who to turn to. The *Webster's American 1828 Dictionary of the English Language* has this to say about the word tribulation: "it often denotes the troubles and distresses which proceed from persecution." But know that this word covers troubles, problems, misfortunes, pain, suffering, harm, and evils. The synonyms to persecution include *harassment*, *opposition*, *torture*, and *torment*.

Unwise choices and decisions bring consequences. As I studied, read, and heard the Word of God being preached, I understood that wise choices could change my life in such a dramatic way. But I also realized that God could even take the unwise choices in my past and use them for His glory.

The unwise choices I had made in my life led me down a path of destruction, beginning with teen premarital sex at the age of fifteen. I ended up dropping out of high school, marrying and divorcing at a very young age, struggling my way through cosmetology school, marrying for a second time and ending that marriage by means of an annulment.

I also endured beatings and mental abuse in both of my marriages, and fighting back in my defense only made things worse. Only the protective hand of God spared my life. Not only did God save me from further injury and death, but He has used each of those circumstances to enable me to understand and help other ladies who are experiencing some of the same challenges in their lives.

When you accept responsibility for the consequences for your own choices, you are on the path to healing. If you are not willing to accept responsibility for your choices, you will never gain victory over bitterness. In fact, you will more than likely continue to make the same bad choices, deepening the hole that you are trying to climb out of.

Another important step in this journey involves forgiving yourself, which is a very important part of forgiving others. Believe me when I say forgiveness is not easy. However, forgiveness does become possible after you accept Christ as your personal Savior. The Bible says in **Matthew 19:26b, "With men this is impossible; but with God all things are possible."** Forgiving others may take some time, and it may take even longer for the restoration of relationships that have been broken. The truth is, some relationships may never be restored.

As a Christian, we are commanded to forgive. The Bible says, **"And be ye kind one to another, tenderhearted, forgiving one another, even as God for Christ's sake hath forgiven you" (Ephesians 4:32).** Although we should hate sin, we must forgive the sinner, even if we do not release him from the penalty of the sin he committed. In other words, if someone has committed a crime against us, we can offer forgiveness even though he still deserves the punishment for his crime. God does not require us to reestablish a relationship with the offender. Forgiveness releases us; it does not release the offender from the penalty of his sin.

I know I struggled for many years to forgive the father of my children. His choice to walk out of our marriage ripped all of our lives apart. Although we remained friends for the sake of our children, I refused to forgive him for his choice to leave. I came to accept most of his behavior; I tolerated him sometimes out of guilt and sometimes out of desperation. Why was I surprised when that marriage ended the way it did? We were both so young and immature when we got married.

The only full recovery from the bondage of bad choices begins with salvation. After salvation, a child of God should accept responsibility for his own choices, learn to forgive himself, and determine to forgive those who hurt him. It wasn't until I accepted Christ as my personal Savior that I understood the magnitude of my sin and recognized how unworthy I was of God's forgiveness, I acknowledged that my debt to God was far greater than this man's debt to me.

In spite of my great sin, God had sweetly and fully forgiven me! *I John 1:9, "If we confess our sins, he is faithful and just to forgive us our sins, and to cleanse us from all unrighteousness."* So with God's help, I was finally able to forgive my first husband, the father of my children.

After giving my second husband, the schizophrenic Prince, an ultimatum, he moved out, and we lived separately for several years before my youngest son and I moved back to California in 1985. My oldest son chose to remain in Arizona since he had a great job and was planning to be married in the near future. My middle son had just graduated from high school and went directly into the Marines. My move to California was going to make it easier for the new Marine to be able to see both parents at the same time.

I had been promised by my ex-husband that I could live in the mother-in-law's quarters behind the main house where he lived until I found a job and could get a place of my own. I arrived in California, only to find out that someone else was living in those quarters, and I would have to wait until she moved out at the end of the month. But... she never moved, so our youngest son and I moved into the main house "temporarily" with my ex-husband and his son from his and his second wife marriage.

Although I did find a job, I did not look for a place of my own because when I left Arizona, I had left all my furniture in the apartment where my oldest son was still living until he got married. As it turned out, one month ran into a few years, and I was still living in the main house. What a situation.

During this time, my ex-husband was estranged from his second wife. After years of an unfaithful relationship, she had permanently walked out on him and their seven-year-old son in the summer of 1984. I found her abandonment to be poetic justice, not knowing at the time what the Bible says in **Galatians 6:7, "Be not deceived; God is not mocked: for whatsoever a man soweth, that shall he also reap."** Later I asked my husband how he had felt when she didn't want to be married anymore. He responded with, "Mad, sad, and rejected." Boy, oh boy could I relate!

During those few years of our living together, my ex-husband asked me to marry him again numerous times, but I repeatedly rejected his offers. The last time he asked me, I gave no answer to his proposal. However, the very next day on my way to work, I made a promise to God, after remembering what His Word said in *2 Corinthians 6:14, "Be ye not unequally yoked together with unbelievers: for what fellowship hath righteousness with unrighteousness? and what communion hath light with darkness?"*

I prayed these words, "Lord, if you want me to marry him, I promise You I will—exactly one year from the day he gets saved." By the word saved, I mean when a person has accepted Christ as his personal Savior. *Unequally yoked* means that the two people involved want to go in different directions, not in agreement.

On February 15, 1990, exactly three days after I had made the promise to God, I came home from work, and my ex-husband's son said, "So, Ma, do you want to hear some good news!?" Well, of course I did. Good news is always welcome, isn't it? "Dad got saved today!" Well, yikes! Who knew that would happen so fast?! I hadn't told a single living soul about that promise I had made to God!

The Holy Spirit who lives within me was talking to me—no, wait, screaming at me. After listening to sermons and being taught the Word of God, I had noticed many things that needed to change in my life. I now realized that my ex-husband and I were living in sin, even though neither of us was married to someone else. Within a month, I had moved in with my younger sister. Not another living soul, except the sister I was now living with, knew about the promise I had made to God. As time drew closer to the day of our getting married, I prayed, "Lord, help me be who I need to be to glorify you."

On Saturday, February 9, 1991, I delivered the news to my ex-husband and two of the boys. I had offered to fix breakfast for them that day just to make sure they were all together when I delivered the news that their dad and I would be getting married in five days—shocking news, I guess, because they all just stared at me. February 15, 1991, exactly one year from my promise to God, all but one of our boys, our daughter-in-law, and two of our granddaughters were present when my ex-husband and I were married for the second time.

My husband's son went to live with his mother on June 10, 1991, a very sad day for us. With his father and me married, his hopes and dreams of that perfect life he had imagined were gone too. Children hold out a hope that their parents will somehow get back together.

Many changes took place in my life as I asked God for wisdom, knowledge, and understanding. I began to grow spiritually and experience a deeper conviction as a result of my sin. The Bible says in ***Isaiah 55:8, "For my thoughts are not your thoughts, neither are your ways my ways, saith the LORD."*** The Bible really brought the truth of my sin home to me with ***Psalm 10:4, "The wicked, through the pride of his countenance, will not seek after God: God is not in all his thoughts."*** Well, who wants to own up to that, huh? It is always such a rude awakening to find out just how easily we can be led astray by the sin of our old habits.

The Lord went to work on me and began to use me in amazing ways when I confessed and turned from my old wicked ways. Who knew that over time God would trust me as a nursery worker, a Sunday school teacher, and a ladies' ministry leader and teacher in my church, but the real shocker to me was being invited as a guest speaker at other churches. God has been so good and very patient with me; in fact, He made this promise found in ***Hebrews 13:5b, "I will never leave thee, nor forsake thee."*** That promise was not made just to me but to every person that has accepted His Son as Savior.

• Questions to think about:

1. Write down the names of people with whom you are angry or against whom you are harboring bitterness.

_____
_____
_____
_____
_____
_____

2. If there are people who are angry or bitter towards you, go to them and get the problem settled by confessing your part and asking them to forgive you. List the names and your offenses against them. (Please note that even if the person refuses to forgive you, you have done what God requires of you.)

_____
_____
_____
_____
_____
_____
_____

- **Verses to memorize:**

    1. *Psalm 51:1-4, "Have mercy upon me, O God, according to thy lovingkindness: according unto the multitude of thy tender mercies blot out my transgressions. Wash me thoroughly from mine iniquity, and cleanse me from my sin. For I acknowledge my transgressions: and my sin is ever before me. Against thee, thee only, have I sinned, and done this evil in thy sight: that thou mightest be justified when thou speakest, and be clear when thou judgest."*

    2. *Proverbs 15:1, "A soft answer turneth away wrath: but grievous words stir up anger."*

    3. *Proverbs 16:7, "When a man's ways please the LORD, he maketh even his enemies to be at peace with him."*

- **Passage to read:**

    Ephesians 5

Chapter 7

A Checklist for Marriage

First of all, there are no perfect marriages! When two people are united in marriage, those two become one, requiring a period of adjusting to each other's ways of thinking and doing. Let's face it. We all have our own idiosyncrasies. Now we have joined our self to someone who has his own preferred ways of doing things contrary to ours, and so the struggles begin....

Know that Satan has, from the beginning of time, set out to destroy homes and families. Here is a list of a few tools that Satan likes to use to destroy a marriage: money, children, drinking, jealousy, in-laws, carousing, selfishness, adultery, lying, denial, and yes, even religion. In reality, the list is endless.

The pastor of the church my husband and I now attend has repeatedly said, "Love is not a feeling; love is a commitment." The Bible says, *"... if a house be divided against itself, that house cannot stand" (Mark 3:25)* and, *"Can two walk together, except they be agreed?" (Amos 3:3).*

I love the book of Proverbs because it has so much to teach us on how to behave in a Godly fashion, which in turn makes for a happy marriage. ***Proverbs 15:6a*** says, *"In the house of* *the righteous is much treasure."* God wants you to have the treasure of a happy marriage.

The Bible identifies the qualities that constitute a good marriage. Notice what the Bible has to say about each of the following characteristics.

• Commitment

Are you truly committed to your marriage under any and all circumstances? The word commitment means "promise." Marriage involves a promise to your spouse and to God. God's commitment to us is found in **Malachi 3:6, "For I am the LORD, I change not...."** So if the Lord never changes, we can trust His never-changing Word, which is the way to true happiness in our marriage.

Matthew 19:6 says, *"Wherefore they are no more twain, but one flesh. What therefore God hath joined together, let not man put asunder."* Commitment is important in your marriage because God is the one who joined the two of you together.

John 15:13 says, *"Greater love hath no man than this, that a man lay down his life for his friends."* So the question is, are you willing to risk or even lose your own life for the sake of your spouse? Or are you the one who would, as the old saying goes, throw your spouse under the bus to save yourself? If you are truly committed, you should be willing to make sacrifices for your spouse.

• Serving

Matthew 11:28-30 says, *"Come unto me, all ye that labour and are heavy laden, and I will give you rest. Take my yoke upon you, and learn of me; for I am meek and lowly in heart: and ye shall find rest unto your souls. For my yoke is easy, and my burden is light."*

Serving covers a lot of area in our marriages. The word *serve* means "to aid, help, assist, support, and succor." *Succor* means "to rescue and to comfort"; *aid* means "to encourage." We are to spend our life serving our spouse, not demanding that our spouse serve us. When we refuse to serve our spouse, we are in reality hurting ourselves because God has joined us together as one. However, by serving our spouse in a quiet, gentle, and humble manner, we are strengthening our marriage and making our own life more peaceful and loving.

Serving with humility is pleasing to God. *Humility* found in the *Webster's Dictionary for Boys and Girls* means "freedom from a proud or haughty manner; meekness." *Meekness* in the same dictionary means "mild-tempered, humble." But to God it means "a willing and submissive spirit."

Proverbs 18:12 says, *"Before destruction the heart of man is haughty, and before honour is humility."* The word *haughty* found in the *Webster's Dictionary for Boys and Girls* means "very proud; inclined to look down on other people; proceeding from or showing great pride; proud." If haughty actions are in your pathway of life, you can be sure—mark it down—destruction is soon to follow.

Proverbs 29:23 says, *"A man's pride shall bring him low: but honour shall uphold the humble in spirit."* Only you can chose between honor and pride in your character.

- ## Forgiveness

We have all offended God and deserve the punishment for our sin. **Galatians 6:7** says, *"Be not deceived; God is not mocked: for whatsoever a man soweth, that shall he also reap."* But in God's love and mercy, He provided forgiveness through His Son Jesus Christ for those who are willing to accept salvation through His death on the Cross. *"For God so loved the world* *that he gave his only begotten Son, that whosoever believeth in him should not perish, but have everlasting life. For God sent not his Son into the world to condemn the world; but that the world through him might be saved" (John 3:16-17).*

Colossians 3:12-1 says, *"Put on therefore, as the elect of God, holy and beloved, bowels of mercies, kindness, humbleness of mind, meekness, longsuffering; Forbearing one another, and forgiving one another, if any man have a quarrel against any: even as Christ forgave you, so also do ye."* Since God is willing to forgive us, we should be willing to forgive others, including our spouse.

Matthew 18:21-22 says, *"Lord, how oft shall my brother sin against me, and I forgive him? till seven times? Jesus saith unto him, I say not unto thee, Until seven times: but, Until seventy times seven."* These verses mean we need to forgive every single time, over and over again, as it is needed. Remember we are forgiving the sinner, not the sin. This may not be easy, but it is very necessary in mending a relationship.

- ## Mercy

Mercy is "an act of kindness and understanding toward another person." It is very easy to demonstrate mercy toward someone you love; for example, a child who did something wrong in innocence. But it is a different story when it comes to having mercy on someone you love who knows what they are doing and continues to partake in their sin and feel justified in doing so, especially when their presumptuous sinful acts are accompanied by the expectancy of your forgiveness without their repentance.

Proverbs 3:3-4 says, *"Let not mercy and truth forsake thee: bind them about thy neck; write them upon the table of thine heart: So shalt thou find favour and good understanding in the sight of God and man."* Mercy is "loving kindness," which is the true meaning of grace. Grace is given even when someone doesn't deserve it. If we keep that in mind and let those qualities be a part of our character, God will see them too.

Matthew 5:7 says, *"Blessed are the merciful: for they shall obtain mercy."* So mercy seems to be a pretty important quality to have in a marriage. However, you will need to call upon the Lord because in many cases mercy and understanding may not come easy for you to bestow on a repeat offender.

- **Purity**

One of the meanings for *purity* in the *Webster's Dictionary for Boys and Girls* is "freedom from guilt or sin; as, *purity* of life." Faithfulness in a marriage is of utmost importance because lost trust is very hard to regain. Trustworthiness is a must because without it a marriage partner will lose all respect, and then happiness flies right out the door.

Adultery starts with a thought and is followed by an action. Proverbs 5 is filled with good instructions and warnings against adultery. Although Proverbs 5 is addressed to a male, the truth also pertains to women.

Proverbs 5:21 and *22* show us something of importance to consider, *"For the ways of man are before the eyes of the LORD, and he pondereth all his goings. His own iniquities shall take the wicked himself, and he shall be holden with the cords of his sins."* This is where forgiveness comes in. It will be very difficult to live with respect for your spouse once that spouse has committed adultery because the marriage bed has been defiled—trust has been broken. However, by the grace of God, with your spouse's repentant heart and your mercy, over time your marriage can be restored.

Hebrews 13:4 says, *"Marriage is honourable in all, and the bed undefiled: but whoremongers and adulterers God will judge."* Purity is the ultimate expression of a lasting love in your marriage.

1 Corinthians 7:3-4 says, "Let the husband render unto the wife due benevolence: and likewise also the wife unto the husband. The wife hath not power of her own body, but the husband: and likewise also the husband hath not power of his own body, but the wife." Because husbands and wives become as one person, disrespecting your spouse is really showing disrespect for yourself. So why would you want to do that? A lack of respect shows a sign of insecurity in you.

• Kindness

Remember how careful you were during your dating relationship? Were you on your best behavior, or was that just a deceitful act? So many times people will portray themselves as kind, considerate, and respectful until they have won their prize, but...once married, they reveal who they really are—mean, inconsiderate and disrespectful. Kindness in a marriage relationship should increase rather than decrease.

Ephesians 4:31-32 says, "Let all bitterness, and wrath, and anger, and clamour, and evil speaking, be put away from you, with all malice: And be ye kind one to another, tenderhearted, forgiving one another, even as God for Christ's sake hath forgiven you." Christ died on the Cross to forgive us of all of our sins. You don't have to die to forgive (though it may feel like it at the time). You just have to find it in your heart to forgive.

Ephesians 4:26 says, "Be ye angry, and sin not: let not the sun go down upon your wrath: Neither give place to the devil." When you and your spouse are disagreeing and an argument is in progress, settle that argument before day's end. You are not going to want Satan to get his foot in the door. Remember that pride comes before destruction and your sin will open the door.

Proverbs 10:12 says, *"Hatred stirreth up strifes: but love covereth all sins."* When you truly love someone and they are having a bad day, it is possible to be kind toward them even when they are not kind toward you. Our words can come easy and land on the hateful side if we are not careful in the middle of an argument. The Bible says, *"A soft answer turneth away wrath: but grievous words stir up anger" (Proverbs 15:1).* Remember, once words are spoken, they cannot be taken back. Will your words be softly spoken in kindness, or will they be words grievously spoken only to be regretted later?

Psalm 19:14 says, *"Let the words of my mouth, and the meditation of my heart, be acceptable in thy sight, O LORD, my strength, and my redeemer."* Remember that God is everywhere, sees everything, hears every word, and you cannot hide anything from Him.

1 Peter 3:4 says, *"But let it be the hidden man of the heart, in that which is not corruptible, even the ornament of a meek and quiet spirit, which is in the sight of God of great price."* In other words, it is very valuable to have a meek and quiet spirit that can be seen not only by man, but also by God. Your true beauty shows from the inside out for all to see.

• **Gratitude**

The *Webster's American 1828 Dictionary of the English Language* states the definition of *gratitude* as follows: "a virtue of the highest excellence, as it implies a feeling and generous heart, and a proper sense of duty." The word *gratitude* was used in the following example sentence: "The love of God is the sublimest *gratitude*." Let your spouse know often how much you appreciate them.

Ephesians 5:33 says, *"Nevertheless let every one of you in particular so love his wife even as himself; and the wife see that she reverence her husband."* I do know this, if the husband is faithful, kind, and loving toward his wife, she will feel cherished and so loved that she will have no problem reverencing her husband. I believe that is where a good marriage starts: loving one another as God loved us.

· Acceptance

Ephesians 1:6-7 says, *"To the praise of the glory of his grace, wherein he hath made us accepted in the beloved. In whom we have redemption through his blood, the forgiveness of sins, according to the riches of his grace."* We are not accepted by our good works, but our good works should be seen by others to bring glory to God. Acceptance of our spouse is crucial to having a loving relationship.

· Availability

Proverbs 31:11-12 says, *"The heart of her husband doth safely trust in her, so that he shall have no need of spoil. She will do him good and not evil all the days of her life."* The wife should always be available when her husband needs her, and vice versa the husband should be there to meet his wife's needs. Marriage should not be a one-sided situation.

Malachi 2:15, "...and let none deal treacherously against the wife of his youth." When married couples do not treat each other with love and respect, problems will eventually occur in every area of their marriage. The word *treacherous* means "deceitful, unfaithful and disloyal," but this could pertain to either spouse, not just the husband. Remember what *Ephesians 4:32* says, *"And be ye kind one to another, tenderhearted, forgiving one another, even as God for Christ's sake hath forgiven you."*

1 Corinthians 7:2 says, *"Nevertheless, to avoid fornication, let every man have his own wife, and let every woman have her own husband."* There are bound to be situations that make one or the other of you want to turn away from your spouse, but you should always be available to each other no matter the circumstances. Of course this is not always easy, but it is necessary or the situation will only get worse. Your choice!

- **Unity**

Psalms 133:1 says, *"Behold, how good and how pleasant it is for brethren to dwell together in unity!"*

Ephesians 4:3 says, *"Endeavoring to keep the unity of the Spirit in the bond of peace."*

Hebrews 13:8 says, *"Jesus Christ the same yesterday, and today, and forever."*

Ephesians 5:1-2 says, *"Be ye therefore followers of God, as dear children; And walk in love, as Christ also hath loved us, and hath given himself for us an offering and a sacrifice to God for a sweetsmelling savour."*

Romans 12:2 says, *"And be not conformed to this world: but be ye transformed by the renewing of your mind, that ye may prove what is that good, and acceptable, and perfect, will of God."*

John 13:17 says, *"If ye know these things, happy are ye if ye do them."* The few Scriptures mentioned above are just a glimpse of what the Word of God has to offer to give guidance as to how to dwell in unity with our spouse for a successful and loving marriage.

Our reputation will beat us to our destination every single time, and it is all about your good name, as the Bible says in *Proverbs 22:1, "A good name is rather to be chosen than*

great riches, and loving favour rather than silver and gold."
A good name cannot be bought. Your name is only as good as you make it. Others are watching you whether you know it or not. Accountability, responsibility, faithfulness—those are biggies that should be on every list of marriage requirements.

- **Questions to think about:**

1. How will a divorce change the course of your life? List the areas of your life that will no doubt be changed by divorce. Don't forget to think about finances, relationships, and the possibility of having to relocate your home, schools, church, even your job. Be as specific as possible.

_____
_____
_____
_____
_____
_____

2. Examine yourself to see if your pride or selfish expectations are part of the problem. Confess any pride and selfishness that the Holy Spirit points out to you. List the areas in which you could personally improve your marriage as the Holy Spirit speaks to you.

_____
_____
_____
_____
_____
_____

Proverbs 2:1-7, "My son, if thou wilt receive my words, and hide my commandments with thee; So that thou incline thine ear unto wisdom, and apply thine heart to understanding; Yea, if thou criest after knowledge, and liftest up thy voice for understanding; If thou seekest her as silver, and searchest for her as for hid treasures; Then shalt thou understand the fear of the LORD, and find the knowledge of God. For the LORD giveth wisdom: out of his mouth cometh knowledge and understanding. He layeth up sound wisdom for the righteous: he is a buckler to them that walk uprightly."

The Plan of Salvation

Do you know God is reaching out to you?

2 Peter 3:9b, "The Lord is…not willing that any should perish, but that all should come to repentance.

He loves you.

John 3:16, "For God so loved the world, that he gave his only begotten Son, that whosoever (you are a whosoever) *believeth in him should not perish,* (go to hell) *but have everlasting life"* (in heaven).

He does not want you to go to hell.

John 3:17, "For God sent not his Son into the world to condemn the world; but that the world through him might be saved."

Romans 3:23, "For all have sinned, and come short of the glory of God."

Romans 6:23, "For the wages of sin is death; but the gift of God is eternal life through Jesus Christ our Lord.

His only begotten Son, Jesus Christ died and rose again to pay for your sin.

Romans 5:8, *"But God commendeth his love toward us, in that, while we were yet sinners, Christ died for us."*

Pray and ask Jesus Christ to be your Savior.

Romans 10:9, *"That if thou shalt confess with thy mouth the Lord Jesus, and shalt believe in thine heart that God hath raised him from the dead, thou shalt be saved."*

I accepted Christ as my personal Savior on:

_____ (Today's date)

Notes:

www.ingramcontent.com/pod-product-compliance
Ingram Content Group UK Ltd.
Pitfield, Milton Keynes, MK11 3LW, UK
UKHW041949230426
12048UKWH00008B/234